Plough Quart

BREAKING GROUND FOR A RENEWED WORLD

Spring 2016, Number 8

Artists: Dean Mitchell, Aristarkh Lentulov, Alex Vogel, Michael D. Fay, Paula Modersohn-Becker, Jennifer Gneiting, Marc Chagall, Vasilij Ivanovic Surikov, Sekino Jun'ichirō

Cover: *Kevin 51*, by Neil Shigley (portfolio on page 21). The artist describes asking Kevin, a homeless man in San Diego, for permission to make his portrait: "I met Kevin near the railroad tracks where there were no businesses and few people. He looked very alone. He pointed to his hospital wristband – perhaps to tell me he was mentally ill. He looked tough and mean from a distance, but up close he seemed the opposite."

WWW.PLOUGH.COM

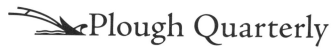

Plough Quarterly

BREAKING GROUND FOR A RENEWED WORLD

www.plough.com

Plough Quarterly features original stories, ideas, and culture to inspire everyday faith and action. Starting from the conviction that the teachings and example of Jesus can transform and renew our world, we aim to apply them to all aspects of life, seeking common ground with all people of goodwill regardless of creed. The goal of *Plough Quarterly* is to build a living network of readers, contributors, and practitioners so that, in the words of Hebrews, we may "spur one another on toward love and good deeds."

This magazine is published by Plough, the publishing house of the Bruderhof, an international movement of Christian communities whose members are called to follow Jesus together in the spirit of the Sermon on the Mount and of the first church in Jerusalem, sharing all talents, income, and possessions (Acts 2 and 4). Bruderhof communities, which include both families and single people from a wide range of backgrounds, are located in the United States, England, Germany, Australia, and Paraguay. Visitors are welcome at any time. To learn more about the Bruderhof's faith, history, and daily life, or to find a community near you to arrange a visit, see *www.bruderhof.com.*

Plough Quarterly includes contributions that we believe are worthy of our readers' consideration, whether or not we fully agree with them. Views expressed by contributors are their own and do not necessarily reflect the editorial position of Plough or of the Bruderhof communities.

Editors: Peter Mommsen, Sam Hine, Maureen Swinger. Art director: Emily Alexander. Online editor: Erna Albertz.
Contributing editors: Timothy Keiderling, Emmy Barth Maendel.
Founding Editor: Eberhard Arnold (1883–1935).

Plough Quarterly No. 8: Who Is My Neighbor?
Published by Plough Publishing House, ISBN 978-0-87486-762-6
Copyright © 2016 by Plough Publishing House. All rights reserved.

Scripture quotations (unless otherwise noted) are from the New Revised Standard Version Bible, copyright © 1989 the Division of Christian Education of the National Council of the Churches of Christ in the United States of America. Used by permission. All rights reserved.

Front cover: Neil Shigley, *Kevin 51,* www.neilshigley.com. Back cover: Sekino Jun'ichirō, *Roof Tiles of Firenze,* color woodblock print33. Los Angeles County Museum of Art. Digital image © 2016 Museum Associates / LACMA. Licensed by Art Resource, NY.

Editorial Office
PO Box 398
Walden, NY 12586
T: 845.572.3455
info@plough.com

Subscriber Services
PO Box 345
Congers, NY 10920-0345
T: 800.521.8011
subscriptions@plough.com

United Kingdom
Brightling Road
Robertsbridge
TN32 5DR
T: +44(0)1580.883.344

Australia
4188 Gwydir Highway
Elsmore, NSW
2360 Australia
T: +61(0)2.6723.2213

Plough Quarterly (ISSN 2372-2584) is published quarterly by Plough Publishing House, PO Box 398, Walden, NY 12586.
Individual subscription $32 per year in the United States; Canada add $8, other countries add $16.
Periodicals postage paid at Walden, NY 12586 and at additional mailing offices.
POSTMASTER: Send address changes to *Plough Quarterly,* PO Box 345, Congers, NY 10920-0345.

Who Is My Neighbor?

Dear Reader,

Across the world, optimism seems to be in notably short supply. From Jordan to Germany, the influx of millions of refugees is straining goodwill to the breaking point. The fact that the newcomers are largely Muslims – and that some are criminals while a few are terrorists – has prompted scaremongering pronouncements that European civilization itself is at risk.

Across the Atlantic, fear of immigrants is also playing a starring role in the US presidential campaign. With months of electioneering still ahead, deep political fissures run through the country – and through many congregations.

You'll be relieved to know that *Plough* won't be offering voting advice. Instead, in this issue we hope to awaken and sharpen the conscience in the light of Jesus' words and example. Our focus here is on the second half of his Great Commandment: Love your neighbor as yourself.

"Who is my neighbor?" These words from Luke 10 are the retort of a young lawyer trying to evade Jesus' call to repentance. Jesus responds by telling the story of the Good Samaritan. He teaches: Your neighbor is no longer defined by nationality, ethnicity, or religion. No, your neighbor is anyone to whom you can do good.

Love of neighbor is not an exalted feeling. It's tough love – tough on oneself, as it means accepting risks and sometimes even suffering. It's the love shown by Syrian Christians and Muslims in Qaryatain (page 6). It's the love shown by the thousands of volunteers who welcome refugees despite growing public hostility. And it's the love that should guide us in an election year:

As citizens, how do we live out love of neighbor in relation to immigrants? To the unborn threatened by abortion, and to their mothers? To prisoners, especially those held in solitary confinement for unconscionable terms and those on death row? To the victims of crime, and to the law enforcement officers charged with keeping the peace? To our youth, who are the ones most gravely harmed by our culture's gender confusion and its godless redefinition of marriage?

On all these fronts and many others, love of neighbor makes claims on us. But there is a place where it truly takes on flesh and blood: in the fellowship of believers, the church. Here love of neighbor can bring about a shared life of mutual care, a reality that Gerhard Lohfink explores on page 38. Here, in fact, our neighbors can become our brothers and sisters. When this happens, we can bear one another's burdens – for example, those of the soldier returning from war (page 52) or of the addict battling a besetting sin (page 60). Amid today's horrors, the church community can become an advance outpost of the great reconciliation to come (2 Cor. 5:17).

Now as never before, many more such outposts are needed.

Warm greetings,

Peter

Peter Mommsen
Editor

Readers Respond

Kuroda Seiki, *Woman Reading*

Editors' Note: *Dozens of readers responded to our editorial in which we affirmed Christian marriage – regardless of recent changes in law – as the lifelong union of one man and one woman (Autumn 2015 issue). Some voiced support; some disagreed vehemently; and others raised important questions. Selected letters and our answers are posted at* plough.com/marriagedebate.

What Do Christians Owe Refugees?

On Plough's Winter 2016 issue, "Mercy": As Christians, we must possess the compassionate heart of Jesus; however, we must also remember we are of another kingdom, the kingdom of God. The nations of this world cannot and will not operate in accordance with the Sermon on the Mount. So I am not critical of national leaders for lacking compassion towards the refugees. However, we as Christians are commanded to honor and love them as people like us, created in God's image.

Joseph Allen Keller, Virginia

Forgiving a Dictator

On Kim Hyun-sik's "Forgiving Kim Jong-il," Winter 2016: This is one of the most moving accounts of forgiveness and reconciliation I have ever read. It is life-transforming. I beg readers to linger over it in prayer. Let us ask God to make us agents of peace in this troubled world.

John Armstrong, Illinois

A Veteran's Legacy

On Maureen Swinger's "Coward, Take My Coward's Hand," Winter 2016: At Christmas, Chris Farlekas used to make as many as a hundred pies in a church kitchen in Middletown, New York, for people who were facing poverty. It was his way of bringing some cheer, however small. In the spirit of what Chris did, this year my family and about ten girls from the Immaculate Heart Academy where I work are going to follow his example. We will be making sixty pies to be distributed to the homeless in New York City. Each pie will have a note attached that simply says, "Love, Chris."

Justin Nadal, New Jersey

Steering the Plough

The more I read *Plough* the more impressed I become. At first I wondered if it was overly American for Brits. But the Winter 2016 issue is truly international, with articles from the Isle of Man, Korea, and Germany. With both a Roman Catholic cardinal and an evangelical like Philip Yancey in the same issue, as well as a letter from a Muslim reader, the ecumenical – indeed multi-faith – range is refreshing.

I always look for short articles suitable for reading at prayers after supper here in our Franciscan Friary – often that's the "Forerunners" biographies at the end such as Mother Maria's or Badshah Khan's. I've also read aloud "Lessons from a Village Cow" by Mahlon Vanderhoof as well as the "From the Archives" excerpt by Laurence Houseman on Saint Francis, which our older brothers could resonate with at once.

As for suggestions, I'd like *Plough* to include more about the Bruderhof communities themselves. And in the Letters section, could you say at least which country letters are from?

Brother Hugh, Society of St Francis, Hilfield Friary, Dorchester, England

---

We welcome letters to the editor. Letters and web comments may be edited for length and clarity, and may be published in any medium. Letters should be sent with the writer's name and address to letters@plough.com.

Evangelicals and Catholics Together

"Howls of negativity" is how J. I. Packer described the reaction of some evangelicals to the launch of Evangelicals and Catholics

ECT founders Colson and Neuhaus

Together (ECT) in 1994: critics saw it as "a subversive Roman Catholic power play." In fact, ECT was founded by Charles Colson and Richard John Neuhaus as a way for Christians from across the Reformation divide to proclaim the gospel together. Since the first ECT statement on Christian unity and mission, eight statements have followed. Some have addressed points of faith such as justification and scripture. Others have spoken to urgent matters of public concern, such as 2006's pro-life declaration and 2012's "In Defense of Religious Freedom."

Last year saw the publication of "The Two Shall Become One: Reclaiming Marriage," ECT's eloquent account of the biblical truth of marriage as the lifelong union of one man and one woman (excerpted in *Plough's* Spring 2015 issue). All nine statements, with introductions and notes, are now available in a valuable volume, *Evangelicals and Catholics Together at Twenty: Vital Statements on Contested Topics* (ed. Timothy George and Thomas G. Guarino, Brazos, 2015). Here is essential reading for anyone concerned about how a divided church can give witness to Jesus together.

Poet in This Issue

Laurie Klein, whose poem "No One Wrings the Air Dry" appears on page 68, is an author and artist who lives in Washington State. Her first poetry collection, *Where the Sky Opens: A Partial Cosmography,* was published in 2015 (Cascade).

The martyrdom of Maria von Monjou, from *Martyrs Mirror*

Bearing Witness

For centuries, Anabaptist communities around the world have been shaped by stories of the martyrs as portrayed in books such as *Martyrs Mirror* and the Hutterian *Chronicle.* These examples of steadfastness unto death still challenge us to faithfulness, repentance, and renewal.

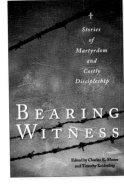

Today, Christian martyrdom is no longer just a distant historical phenomenon; thousands of Christians die for their faith each year, many of them members of Anabaptist congregations such as the Nigerian Christians persecuted by Boko Haram. In the tradition of *Martyrs Mirror,* the Bearing Witness Stories Project has been collecting their stories at *www.martyrstories.org* and now in a new book, *Bearing Witness: Stories of Martyrdom and Costly Discipleship* (Plough, 2016). In the words of J. Nelson Kraybill, president of the Mennonite World Conference: "Christian martyrdom and costly discipleship are not confined to some legendary past. This book teaches us about nonviolent love in the face of opposition and challenge us to take risks for the gospel today."

Love in Syria

Learning from Jacques Mourad

NAVID KERMANI

SYRIA AND IRAQ, persecuted Middle Eastern Christians, the true nature of Islam: in a controversial speech in October 2015 upon accepting the Peace Prize of the German Book Trade in Frankfurt, the Muslim writer Navid Kermani tackled a host of contested questions. And he asked: Will Western Christians respond, or stay indifferent?

On the same day that I learned I had been awarded the Peace Prize of the German Book Trade, Jacques Mourad was abducted in Syria. Two armed men entered the Mar Elian monastery on the outskirts of the small town of Qaryatain and called for Father Jacques. They found him, likely in the bare little office that also serves as his living room and bedroom and took him away. On May 21, 2015, Jacques Mourad became a hostage of the so-called Islamic State (ISIS).

I first met Father Jacques in autumn 2012 when I was traveling as a journalist through an already war-torn Syria. He served Qaryatain's Catholic parish while also belonging to the religious order of Mar Musa, which was founded in the early 1980s in a derelict early Christian monastery. This order is a special, even unique Christian community, since it is devoted to an encounter with Islam and to love for Muslims. The monks and nuns, while conscientiously holding to the Catholic Church's precepts and rites, engage just as seriously with Islam and take part in Muslim traditions, including Ramadan. This may sound mad, even ludicrous: Christians who, in their own

words, have fallen in love with Islam. And yet this Christian–Muslim love was a reality in Syria until just recently, and remains so still in the hearts of many Syrians. Through the work of their hands, the goodness of their hearts, and the prayers of their souls, the nuns and monks of Mar Musa created a place that to me seemed a utopia, a place where the eschatological reconciliation of all things was – well, perhaps not already fulfilled (they would not have claimed this), but still tangible in advance as a promise of the reconciliation to come.

This was the Mar Musa I came to know: a seventh-century stone monastery amid the overpowering solitude of the mountains of the Syrian desert, a place visited not only by Christians from all over the world but also by ever-increasing numbers of Muslims, who knocked at the door to meet their Christian brothers and sisters; to speak, sing, and be silent with them; and also, in a corner of the church kept free of images, to pray according to their Islamic custom.

When I visited Father Jacques in 2012, his friend Paolo Dall'Oglio, the Italian Jesuit who had founded the Mar Musa community,

Opposite, Mar Musa monastery, 2008; the cable stretching across the valley to the building is to transport firewood.

Navid Kermani is an Iranian German writer and journalist who lives in Cologne. This translation from the German, newly revised for Plough, *is based on its first publication in "Friedenspreis des Deutschen Buchhandels 2015", ed. Börsenverein des Deutschen Buchhandels (Frankfurt am Main, 2015).*

had recently been expelled from the country. Father Paolo had been too outspoken in his criticism of the Assad government, which had responded to the Syrian people's call for freedom and democracy – a call that had remained peaceful for nine months – with arrests and torture, with truncheons and assault rifles, and finally with horrific massacres and even poison gas until the country descended into civil war. But Father Paolo had also confronted the leadership of the official Syrian churches, which remained silent about the government's violence. He had attempted in vain to persuade Europe to support Syria's democracy movement and had called in vain on the United Nations to impose a no-fly zone or at least send observers. He had warned in vain of a religious war if the secular and moderate groups were abandoned and foreign aid went only to the jihadists. He had tried in vain to break through the wall of our apathy. In the summer of 2013, the founder of the Mar Musa community secretly returned to Syria to help recover some Muslim friends who were in the hands of ISIS, and was himself abducted by its forces. There has been no trace of Father Paolo Dall'Oglio since July 28, 2013.

Father Jacques, now responsible for the Mar Elian monastery in Dall'Oglio's absence, is very different in character: not a gifted orator, not a man of charisma, not a passionate Italian, but rather, like so many Syrians I met, a proud, thoughtful, and extremely polite man, quite tall, with a broad face, his short hair still black. I did not get to know him well, of course; I attended Mass, which consisted of

> "We Christians are a part of Syria. Arab culture is our culture!"
>
> Jacques Mourad

enchantingly beautiful singing as in all Eastern churches, and observed how warmly he chatted to the faithful and to local dignitaries at the subsequent lunch. After farewelling all the guests, he led me to his tiny room and placed a chair for me next to the narrow bed upon which he sat for the half-hour interview.

It was not only his words that amazed me – how fearlessly he criticized the government, and how openly he also spoke of the hardening in his own Christian community. What made an even more profound impression on me was his demeanor: I experienced him as a quiet, very conscientious, introspective, and ascetic servant of God who, now that God had given him the task of caring for the beleaguered Christians in Qarya-tain and leading the monastic community, was carrying out this public duty with all his might. He spoke quietly and so slowly – often with his eyes closed – that it was as if he were consciously slowing down his pulse and using the interview as a time to rest between other, more strenuous commit-ments. Yet he chose his words with great care and articulated his thoughts in press-ready sentences. What he said was of such clarity and political incisiveness that I kept asking whether it might not be too dangerous to quote him verbatim. Then he opened his warm, dark eyes and nodded wearily – yes, he said, I could print everything, otherwise he would not have said it. The world had to learn what was happening in Syria.

This weariness was perhaps my strongest impression of Father Jacques – it was the weariness of one who had not only realized but indeed had consented to the fact that he might never rest until the next life. It was, too,

Jacques
Mourad

the weariness of a doctor or a firefighter who rations his energy when the emergency becomes overwhelming. And Father Jacques was indeed a doctor and a firefighter in the midst of the war, not only for the souls of those living in fear, but also for the bodies of the needy to whom he offered food, protection, clothes, accommodation, and, above all, compassion in his church, regardless of their religion. Many hundreds if not thousands of refugees, the vast majority of them Muslims, were given shelter at the monastery and provided for by the community of Mar Musa. And not only that: Father Jacques managed to maintain peace, including peace between the religions, at least in Qaryatain. It is chiefly thanks to him – the quiet, serious Father Jacques – that the different groups and militias, some allied with the government and others with the opposition, agreed to ban all heavy weapons from the town. And he, the priest who was critical of the official Syrian church, succeeded in persuading almost all the Christians in his parish to stay. "We Christians are a part of this country, even if the fundamentalists here and in Europe don't like to hear it," Father Jacques told me. "Arab culture is our culture!"

He reacted with some bitterness to the calls of certain Western politicians to take in only Christian Arabs. The same West that had failed to lift a finger for the millions of Syrians of all faiths who had demonstrated peacefully for democracy and human rights, the same West that had devastated Iraq and supplied Assad with his poison gas, the same West that remained an ally of Saudi Arabia, the main sponsor of jihadism – this same West was now concerned about the Arab Christians? The very idea made him laugh, said Father Jacques,

unsmilingly. He continued with his eyes closed: "With such irresponsible statements, these politicians add fuel to the religious hatred that threatens us Christians."

Father Jacques's responsibilities grew constantly, and he bore them without complaint. The monastic community's foreign members had to leave Syria and take refuge in northern Iraq. The seven Syrian monks and nuns who remained divided themselves between the two monasteries of Mar Musa and Mar Elian. Since the battlefronts were constantly shifting, Qaryatain was sometimes ruled by the Syrian government and sometimes by opposition militias. The monks and nuns had to come to terms with both sides and, like their fellow citizens, endure government bombing attacks whenever the town was in the hands of the opposition. Things changed, however, as ISIS advanced ever deeper into the Syrian heartland. "The threat from ISIS, this cult of terrorists who present a ghastly image of Islam, has arrived in our region," Father Jacques wrote to a French friend a few days before his abduction. "It is difficult to decide what we should do. Should we leave our homes? To us that seems very hard. The realization that we have been abandoned is dreadful – abandoned especially by the Christian world, which has decided to keep its distance so that the danger will stay far away. We mean nothing to them."

Mosaic roof in the Nabi Habeel Mosque, Syria

Just in these few lines of a hastily written email, two parts stand out that are characteristic of Father Jacques. The first one is the sentence beginning: "The threat from ISIS, this cult of terrorists who present a ghastly image of Islam . . . " The second one concerns the Christian world: "We mean nothing to them." He defended the other faith community while criticizing his own. Just as a group claiming to represent Islam and to be applying the requirements of the Quran was physically threatening him and his community directly, and just a few days before his abduction, Father Jacques still insisted that these terrorists were distorting the true face of Islam.

Now, I would disagree with any Muslim whose only response to the Islamic State is the worn-out protest that violence has nothing to do with Islam. But here was a Christian – and a priest at that – who when faced with the possibility of being expelled, humiliated, abducted, or killed by followers of another faith still insisted on justifying that same faith. Such a servant of God displays an inner greatness that I have only encountered in the lives of the saints.

Someone like me cannot, and may not, defend Islam in this way. Love of one's own – one's own culture, one's own country, and equally one's own person – proves itself in self-criticism. The love of the other – of another person, another culture, and even another religion – can be far more effusive and unreserved. It is true that the prerequisite for love of the other is love of oneself. But one can only be in love with something, as Father Paolo and Father Jacques are in love with Islam, if it is the other. Self-love, on the other hand, if it is to avoid falling prey to narcissism, self-praise, or self-satisfaction, must be a struggling, doubting, and ever-questioning love. How true that is of Islam today! Any Muslim who does not struggle with it, doubt it, and question it critically does not love Islam.

It's not only the horrific news and the even more horrific pictures from Syria and Iraq, where the Quran is held aloft during every atrocity and *Allahu akbar* is called out at every beheading. In so many other countries in the Muslim world, Islam is invoked by state authorities, quasi-governmental institutions, theological schools, and rebel groups alike when they oppress their own people, disadvantage women, and persecute, drive out, or massacre those who think, live, or believe differently. Islam is invoked when women are stoned in Afghanistan, when entire school classes are murdered in Pakistan, when hundreds of girls are enslaved in Nigeria, when Christians are beheaded in Libya, when bloggers are shot in Bangladesh, when marketplaces are bombed in Somalia, when Sufis and musicians are murdered in Mali, when critics of the regime are crucified in Saudi Arabia, when the best contemporary literature is banned in Iran, when Shiites are oppressed in Bahrain, and when Sunnis and Shiites murder each other in Yemen.

> "We have been abandoned by the Christian world. We mean nothing to them."
>
> Jacques Mourad

To be sure, most Muslims reject terror, violence, and oppression. This is not just an empty talking point, but rather a reality I have experienced directly on my travels. Those who cannot take freedom for granted learn most poignantly to appreciate its value. All the mass uprisings in the Islamic world in recent years were uprisings for democracy and human rights. That includes not only the attempted (and mostly failed) revolutions in nearly all Arab countries, but also the protest movements in Turkey, Iran, and Pakistan, as well as the revolt at the ballot box in the last Indonesian presidential election. It is likewise instructive to note where the streams of Muslim refugees are headed in their hope to find better lives: it's certainly not to religious dictatorships. Meanwhile, the reports that reach us from Mosul or Raqqa hardly testify to popular enthusiasm for the ISIS occupiers, but instead to panic and despair. Every significant theological authority in the Islamic world has rejected ISIS's claim to speak for Islam, documenting in detail how its practices and ideology go against the Quran and the fundamental tenets of Islamic theology. Let us not forget either that those on the frontlines in the battle against the Islamic State are themselves Muslims – Kurds and Shiites, as well as Sunni tribes and the soldiers of the Iraqi army.

All of this needs to be said to puncture the fiction being promoted equally by Islamists and by Islam's critics, both using identical words: that Islam is waging a war against the West. Rather, Islam is waging a war against itself. That is to say, the Islamic world is being shaken by an internal conflict whose effects on the political and ethnic cartography may well match those that resulted from the upheavals of World War I. The multiethnic, multireligious, and multicultural Orient whose magnificent literary productions from the Middle Ages I studied; the Orient that I learned to love during long stays in Cairo and Beirut, childhood summer holidays in Isfahan, and visits at the monastery of Mar Musa; the Orient that, although always endangered and never free of maladies, nevertheless remained a living reality: this Orient will cease to exist, just like the pre–World War I Europe which the German poet Stefan Zweig looked back on with nostalgia and grief in the 1920s.

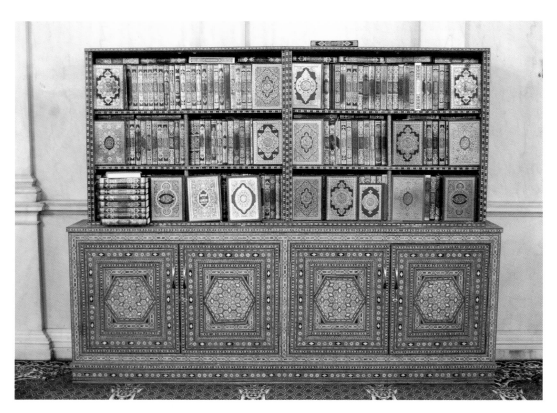

Bookcase in the Umayyad Mosque, Damascus

What happened? ISIS was not born just yesterday, nor did it start with the civil wars inIraq and Syria. Much as its methods might meet with disapproval, its ideology, Wahhabism, is a movement whose influence extends to the furthest corners of the Islamic world today and which, in the form of Salafism, has become especially attractive to young people in Europe. The fact that the schoolbooks and curricula used by ISIS are 95 percent identical to those used in Saudi Arabia indicate that it's not only in Iraq and in Syria that the world is starkly divided into "forbidden" and "permitted," or where humanity is divided into believers and unbelievers. For decades, thanks to billions of dollars of sponsorship from the oil industry, a worldview has been promoted in mosques, in books, and on television that declares all who hold different beliefs to be heretics – reviling, terrorizing, slandering, and insulting them. Once it's become a habit to systematically

denigrate others day after day, it's only consistent – how well we know this from our own German history! – to end up declaring their lives worthless too. That this religious fascism has even become conceivable, that ISIS finds so many fighters and even more sympathizers, that this organization has been able to overrun entire countries and capture cities of millions with minimal resistance – all this represents not the beginning, but rather the tentative endpoint of a long deterioration, especially a deterioration of the religious imagination.

I became a student of Middle Eastern Studies in 1988; my topics were the Quran and poetry. Any who study this subject in its classical form soon reach a point where they can no longer reconcile the past with the present. And they become hopelessly sentimental. Of course, the past was not only a peaceful and motley rainbow. As a philologist, however, I focused on the writings of mystics, philosophers, rhetoricians, and theologians. Like other students of this literature, I can only marvel at the originality, intellectual scope, aesthetic power, and sheer humanity we find in the spirituality of Ibn Arabi, the poetry of Rumi, the historiography of Ibn Khaldun, the poetic theology of Abd al-Qahir al-Jurjani, the philosophy of Averroës, the travel reports of Ibn Battuta, and indeed the tales of *One Thousand and One Nights,* which are worldly – yes, worldly and erotic, and incidentally feminist too – while yet being infused throughout with the spirit and language of the Quran. Admittedly, this great literature is not journalistic reporting, and no doubt the social reality of this advanced civilization, like the reality of any age, was much darker and more violent. Yet these literary witnesses tell us what was once conceivable, even self-evident, within Islam. None of this, nothing at all, is to be found in the religious culture of modern Islam – nothing that is even remotely comparable in depth or power of fascination to the writings I came across during my studies. And this is to say nothing of Islamic architecture, Islamic art, or Islamic musical culture; these no longer exist.

To give an illustration of this loss of creativity and freedom taken from my own field, literature: it was once thinkable, even self-evident, that the Quran should be approached as a poetic text, one to be understood using the tools and methods of poetry scholarship: that is, as a poem. It was thinkable, even self-evident, that to be a Muslim theologian also meant being a literary scholar and a connoisseur of poetry; in many cases, the theologian was himself a poet. Yet in our day my own teacher, Nasr Hamid Abu Zaid in Cairo, was charged

with heresy, fired from his university post, and even forced to divorce his wife because he understood Quranic scholarship as a form of literary scholarship. Thus an approach to the Quran which had long been taken as a given and which, as Nasr Abu Zaid pointed out, was used by the most important scholars of classical Islamic theology, has today been defined as unthinkable. Anyone who approaches the Quran in this undoubtedly traditional way is persecuted, punished, and declared a heretic.

In reality, the Quran is poetry not just because the lines rhyme, but also because it speaks in disturbing and enigmatic images with multiple meanings; it is less a book than a recitation, the score of a song that moves its Arab listeners with its rhythms, onomatopoeia, and melodies. Islamic theology not only used to recognize the Quran's aesthetic qualities but went even further, declaring its literary beauty to be the authenticating miracle of Islam. By contrast, today we can observe all over the Islamic world what happens when one ignores or fails to understand the linguistic structure of a text. The Quran is degraded to a how-to manual that can be word-searched for this or that catch phrase. The Quran's literary power thus becomes political dynamite.

It's often claimed that Islam must pass through the fire of enlightenment or that modernity must win out over tradition. But that seems simplistic considering that Islam's past is so much more enlightened than its present and its traditional writings often appear more modern than its current

> **The Quran is less a book than the score of a song that moves its Arab listeners with its music, onomatopoeia, and melodies.**

theological discourse. After all, Islamic culture fascinated Goethe, Proust, Lessing, and Joyce – hardly an indication of a lack of enlightenment. In Islam's books and monuments these writers saw something that we, who are so often brutally confronted by Islam's present state, no longer can easily perceive. Perhaps the problem of Islam is not tradition, but rather the near-total break with tradition – Islam's loss of cultural memory, its civilizational amnesia.

Modernization as experienced by each of the peoples of the Orient was imposed brutally from above, through colonialism and secular dictatorships. Iranian women, for example, did not let go of the headscarf gradually; instead, in 1936 the Shah sent his soldiers out into the streets to tear it from their heads by force. Unlike in Europe, where people experienced modernity (despite various setbacks and crimes) as a process of emancipation that spanned decades and centuries, in the Middle East modernization was largely an experience of violence. Modernity is thus linked not with freedom, but with exploitation and despotism.

Imagine an Italian president driving a car into Saint Peter's Basilica, jumping onto the altar with his dirty boots, and striking the Pope in the face with his whip – then you will have a rough idea of what it meant when, in 1928, Reza Shah marched through the holy shrine of Qom, Iran, in his riding boots and responded to the imam's request to take off his shoes like any other believer by striking him in the face with his whip. You would find comparable events and key moments in other countries across the Middle East, countries that did not detach themselves slowly from the past but rather sought to raze the past and erase it from memory.

Surely, one might have thought, the religious fundamentalists who gained influence throughout the Islamic world after the failure of nationalism would value their own culture. Yet the opposite was the case: by seeking to return to a legendary state of original purity, they not only neglected Islamic tradition but zealously fought against it. ISIS's acts of iconoclasm will be surprising only to those unaware that in Saudi Arabia there are virtually no ancient relics left. In Mecca, the Wahhabis destroyed the graves and mosques of the Prophet's closest kin and even his house of birth. The historic mosque of the Prophet in Medina has been replaced with a gigantic new construction, and on the spot where, until a few years ago, the house still stood that was home to Mohammed and his wife Khadija, you will now find public toilets.

> The Kaaba, the holiest place in Islam, this plain yet magnificent edifice, is literally overshadowed by Gucci and Apple.

Aside from the Quran, my studies focused mainly on Islamic mysticism, that is, Sufism. *Mysticism* may sound marginal and esoteric, a kind of underground culture. In the context of Islam, nothing could be further from the truth. Well into the twentieth century, Sufism formed the basis of popular religion almost everywhere in the Islamic world; in Asian Islam, it still does. At the same time, the spirit of mysticism pervaded Islamic high culture, especially poetry, visual art, and architecture. As the most common form of religious practice, Sufism served as the ethical and aesthetic counterweight to the orthodoxy of the legal scholars. Emphasizing God's compassion above all and finding it behind every letter of the Quran, Sufism always sought beauty in religion and acknowledged the truth in other forms of faith, expressly adopting the Christian commandment to love one's enemies. In this way, Sufism infused Islamic societies with values, stories, and sounds that literalistic forms of devotion could never have supplied. As a lived Islam, Sufism did not negate legal Islam but rather broadened it, rendering its everyday form gentler, more ambivalent, more porous, more tolerant, and especially – through music, dance and poetry – more open to sensual experience.

Very little of this has survived. Wherever the Islamists gained a foothold, starting in nineteenth-century Arabia and continuing up to their recent seizure of power in Mali, they have begun by banning Sufi holy days, prohibiting the mystical writings, destroying the graves of the saints, and cutting off the long hair of the Sufi leaders (or simply killing them). And it hasn't been just the Islamists. The reformers and religious modernizers of the nineteenth and early twentieth centuries also viewed the traditions and customs of popular Islam as backward and antiquated. Given their failure to appreciate Sufi literature, it fell to Western scholars such as the Orientalist Annemarie Schimmel, winner of the 1995 Peace Prize, to edit Sufi manuscripts and save them from destruction. Even today, only a handful of Muslim intellectuals engage with the riches found in their own tradition. The historic city centers all over the Islamic world – damaged, neglected, strewn with rubbish, and filled with ruined monuments – symbolically represent the decline of the Islamic spirit.

So does the largest shopping mall in the world, built in Mecca right next to the Kaaba. You have to see the photos to believe it: the Kaaba, the holiest place in Islam, this plain yet magnificent edifice, is literally overshadowed by Gucci and Apple. Perhaps we should have paid less attention to the Islam of our grand theorists, and more to the Islam of our grandmothers.

To be sure, in some countries historic buildings and mosques are being restored, but this has happened only after Western art historians or westernized Muslims like me recognized the value of the tradition. Unfortunately we arrived at the scene a century too late, when the buildings had already crumbled, the architectural techniques had been forgotten, and the books had been erased from memory. Yet we believed that at least there would be time for thorough study of these things. Instead, I now feel much like an archaeologist in a war zone, hastily and unmethodically gathering up relics so that later generations will at least be able to view them in museums. Certainly Muslim countries are still producing outstanding works of art, as is evident at *biennales,* film festivals, and here at the Frankfurt Book Fair. But this culture has precious little to do with Islam. There is no longer an Islamic culture, at least none of quality. What we now find flying around us and falling on our heads is the wreckage of a massive intellectual implosion.

I s there any hope? There is hope until the last breath – this is what Father Paolo Dall'Oglio, founder of Mar Musa, teaches us. Hope is the central motif in his writings. The day after Father Jacques, Dall'Oglio's pupil and deputy, was abducted, the Muslims of Qaryatain flooded into the church unasked in order to pray for him. That must surely give us hope that love crosses the boundaries between religions, ethnicities, and cultures. The shock created by the news and images of ISIS is immense and has released opposing forces. At long last, within Islamic orthodoxy there is growing resistance to violence in the name of religion. In addition, over the last few years we've witnessed the emergence of a new mode of religious thought, perhaps less in the Arabian heartland of Islam than on its peripheries in Asia, South Africa, Iran, Turkey, and (not least) among Muslims in the West. This process is similar to Europe's re-creation of itself after the two World Wars.

Perhaps I should mention at this juncture Europe's project of unification, which – despite the frivolousness, superficiality, and even open despisal shown toward it by our politicians and by us as a society – remains the most valuable political achievement of this continent. How often on my travels people mention Europe to me as a model, almost a utopia. Anyone who has forgotten why there needs to be a Europe should look at the gaunt, exhausted, frightened faces of the refugees who have left everything behind, given up everything, and risked their lives for the promise that Europe still represents.

That brings me back to the second of Father Jacques's statements that I found remarkable, namely his comment about the Christian world's attitude to him and his Syrian neighbors: "We mean nothing to them." As a Muslim, it is not my place to reproach the Christians of the world for their unconcern, whether toward the Syrian or Iraqi peoples in general, or toward their brothers and sisters in the faith in particular. And yet such reproaches are hard to suppress when I see the public indifference in our country to the truly apocalyptic disaster playing out in the Middle East, one which we try to keep at bay with barbed wire fences, warships, bogeymen, and mental blinkers.

Only three hours' flight from Frankfurt, entire ethnic groups are being exterminated or expelled, girls are being enslaved, many of humanity's most important cultural monuments are being blown up by barbarians, and cultures are disappearing, taking with them an ancient ethnic, religious, and linguistic diversity that, unlike in Europe, had still partly persisted into the twenty-first century. Yet we do not band together and stand up until this war strikes us here, as it did in Paris, or when the people fleeing from this war come knocking at our gates.

It is a good thing that – unlike after September 11, 2001 – our societies have opposed terror with freedom. It is exhilarating to see how so many people in Europe, especially Germany, are supporting refugees. But too often, this protest and this solidarity remain apolitical. We are not having a broad debate in our society about the causes of terror and of the movement of refugees, or about how our own policies may be exacerbating the disaster taking place near our borders. We do not ask why our closest partner in the Middle East is Saudi Arabia, of all countries. We do not

> The day after Father Jacques was abducted, the Muslims of Qaryatain flooded into the church to pray for him.

BUSINESS REPLY MAIL

FIRST-CLASS MAIL   PERMIT NO. 332   CONGERS, NY

POSTAGE WILL BE PAID BY ADDRESSEE

PLOUGH QUARTERLY
PO BOX 345
CONGERS NY 10920-9895

learn from our mistakes when we roll out the red carpet for a dictator like General el-Sisi. Or we learn the wrong lessons, such as when we conclude from the disastrous wars in Iraq and Libya that it is best to stay uninvolved even when a genocide is underway. We still have no idea how to prevent the murder being committed by the Syrian regime against its own people for the last four years. Similarly, we have seemingly come to terms with the existence of a new religious fascism that controls a territory roughly as big as Great Britain, extending from the Iranian border almost to the Mediterranean.

Clearly there are no simple answers to such questions as how to liberate a city of millions like Mosul – but we do not even pose the question seriously. Yet for the community of nations, an organization like ISIS with its estimated thirty thousand fighters is not invincible – we must not allow it to be. "Today they are with us," said the Catholic bishop of Mosul, Yohanna Petros Mouche, when he begged for help from the West and other global powers to drive ISIS out of Iraq. "Today they are with us. Tomorrow they will be with you."

I'd rather not imagine what more will have to happen before we heed the bishop of Mosul's warning. After all, it is part of ISIS's propagandistic logic to create ever higher levels of horror so that its images penetrate our consciousness. As soon as we were no longer outraged to see individual Christian hostages saying the rosary before being beheaded, ISIS started beheading entire groups of Christians. When we banished the decapitations from our screens, ISIS burnt the artwork at the National Museum in Mosul. Once we had grown used to the sight of smashed statues, ISIS began leveling whole ruined cities like Nimrod and Nineveh. When the expulsions of Yazidis had ceased to interest us, the news of mass rapes

The Sayyidah Zainab Mosque, Syria

briefly jolted us from our slumber. When we thought the terrors were limited to Iraq and Syria, snuff videos reached us from Libya and Egypt. After we had become accustomed to the beheadings of some and the crucifixions of others, the victims were first beheaded and then crucified, as recently occurred in Libya. Palmyra is not being blown up all at once, but is being destroyed edifice by edifice at intervals of several weeks so that each time there will be a fresh news item.

This will not stop. ISIS will keep escalating the horror until we see, hear, and feel in our everyday European lives that this horror will not stop by itself. Paris will only have been the beginning, and the decapitation in Lyons will not be the last. The longer we wait, the fewer options remain. In other words, it is already far too late.

Can the winner of a peace prize call for war? I am not calling for war. I am simply pointing out that there is a war – and that we too, as its close neighbors, must respond to it, possibly by military means, yes, but above all with far more determination than has so far been shown either by diplomats or by civil society. For this war can no longer be ended only in Syria and Iraq. It can be ended only by the powers behind the warring armies and militias: Iran, Turkey, the Gulf states, Russia, and (not least) the West. And only when our societies no longer accept the madness will governments make a move. Whatever we do at this point, we will probably make mistakes. But our greatest mistake would be to do nothing or too little against the mass murder being carried out by ISIS and the Assad regime at Europe's doorstep.

"I have just returned from Aleppo," Father Jacques continued in the email he wrote a few days before his abduction on May 21, "this city that sleeps by the river of pride, which lies at the center of the Orient. It is now like a woman who is consumed by cancer. Everyone is fleeing from Aleppo, especially the poor Christians. Yet these massacres don't only harm the Christians; they harm the entire Syrian people. Our vocation is hard to live out, especially in these days after the disappearance of Father Paolo, the twenty-first century's preeminent teacher and initiator of dialogue. Right now, the kind of dialogue we're experiencing is our shared suffering as a community. We are sorrowing in this unjust world, which bears a share of the responsibility for the victims of the war, this world of the dollar and the euro, which cares only for its own citizens, its own wealth, and its own safety while the rest of the world dies of hunger, sickness, and war. It seems that its only aim is to find regions where it can wage wars and further increase its sales of armaments and airplanes. How do these governments justify themselves when they could end the massacres but do nothing, nothing? I do not fear for my faith, but I fear for the world. The question we ask ourselves is this: do we have the right to live or not? The answer has already been given, for this war is a clear answer, as clear as the sun's light. So the true dialogue we are living today is the dialogue of compassion. Courage, my dear, I am with you and hold you tight, Jacques."

On July 28, 2015, two months after the abduction of Father Jacques, ISIS captured the small town of Qaryatain. The majority of the population managed to escape at the last moment, but two hundred Christians were kidnapped. A month later, on August 21, the monastery of Mar Elian was destroyed by bulldozers. From the pictures that ISIS posted online, it seems that not one of the 1,700-year-old stones was left standing. Another two weeks later, on September 3, an ISIS-affiliated website posted photos showing some of the Christians from Qaryatain sitting in the front rows of a school auditorium or event hall, their heads shaven, some of them barely more than skin and bones, with empty gazes, all of them marked by their captivity. Father Jacques can also be identified on the photos, wearing plain clothes, likewise gaunt and with a shaved head, the distress clearly visible in his eyes. He is covering his mouth with his hand, as if unwilling to believe what he is seeing. On the stage of the hall one sees a broad-shouldered, long-bearded man in combat gear signing a contract. It is what is known as a dhimmi contract, which subjects Christians to Muslim rule. Christians are forbidden to build churches or monasteries or to carry a cross or Bible with them. Their priests cannot wear clerical attire. Muslims are not allowed to hear the prayers of the Christians, read their writings, or enter their churches. Christians cannot bear arms and must submit unconditionally to the directives of the Islamic State. They must bow their heads, endure every injustice without complaint, and pay a special poll tax, the *jizya*, if they are to live. It churns the stomach to read this contract: it blatantly divides God's creatures into first-class and second-class humans, and leaves no doubt that there are also humans of a third class whose lives are worth even less.

It is a calm, but utterly depressed and helpless gaze we see in Father Jacques's face on the photo as he covers his mouth with his hand. He had reckoned with his own martyrdom. But to see his parish taken hostage – the children he christened, the lovers he married, the elderly to whom he promised the final sacramental unction – must be enough to make him lose his mind, to make even a man so thoughtful, so inwardly strong, and so God-loving as Father Jacques lose his mind. After all, it was on his account that his fellow hostages had stayed in Qaryatain rather than fleeing Syria like so many other Christians. Father Jacques no doubt believes that he has incurred guilt, but I know this much: God will judge him differently.

The Mar Elian monastery before, during, and after its destruction by ISIS forces in August 2015. These stills were taken from an ISIS video.

I s there hope? Yes, there is hope. There is always hope. I had already written this speech when I received the news that Father Jacques Mourad is free. Citizens of the town of Qaryatain helped to liberate him from jail, then disguised him and brought him out of ISIS territory with the help of Bedouins. He has now returned to his brothers and sisters in the Mar Musa community. Obviously, a number of people were involved in the rescue operation, all of them Muslim; each one of them risked their life for a Christian priest. Love has prevailed over the borders of religions, ethnicities, and culture.

And yet, as magnificent as this news is – indeed, as wondrous as it is in the very sense of the word – our worry must nevertheless outweigh our joy, especially our worry for Father Jacques himself. Indeed, the lives of the two hundred other Christians in Qaryatain are likely now in even greater danger than before his liberation. And there is still no trace of his teacher, Father Paolo, the founder of the Christian community that loves Islam. But there is hope until our last breath.

The winner of a peace prize should not call for war. But he can call to prayer. Ladies and gentlemen, I would like to make an unusual request – though it is not really so unusual in a church. I would like you to refrain from applauding at the end of my speech and instead pray for Father Paolo and the two hundred kidnapped Christians of Qaryatain, for the children baptized by Father Jacques, for the lovers he married, and for the elderly to whom he promised the sacrament of anointing. And if you are not religious, let your wishes be with those who have been abducted, and with Father Jacques, who must struggle with the fact that only he was freed. For what are

> The winner of a peace prize should not call for war. But he can call to prayer.

prayers but wishes addressed to God? I believe in wishes and believe that they have an effect on our world, with or without God. Without wishes, humanity would never have laid the stones on top of one another that it so recklessly destroys in its wars. And so I ask you, ladies and gentlemen, to pray for Jacques Mourad, pray for Paolo Dall'Oglio, pray for the abducted Christians of Qaryatain, pray or wish for the liberation of all hostages and the freedom of Syria and Iraq. You are welcome to stand up too, so that we can oppose the snuff videos of the terrorists by presenting a picture of our fraternity. ⟶

In December 2015, Father Jacques Mourad, who had traveled to Europe after his escape from ISIS, announced he would soon return to Syria: "I have no fear, God will hold his hand over me."

Navid Kermani leads his audience in prayer for Iraq and Syria.

"An intolerable affront" was how one German newspaper described Navid Kermani's gesture in closing his October 2015 speech (above) with a call for his hearers to join him in praying for ISIS's Christian victims. As Kermani, a Muslim, lifted his hands in prayer, his one thousand listeners—some, no doubt, to their own surprise—rose to join him. In the media furor that followed, prominent commentators accused Kermani of manipulating his audience. Some pundits even linked Kermani's "politicized" prayer to the theocratic ideology of ISIS.

Though many others rose to Kermani's defense, it was a telling moment. Will it take Muslim voices like Kermani's to remind the post-Christian West of its own spiritual roots? Surely the answer to ISIS's evil is not a God-free public square, but rather the same love that inspired both Jacques Mourad and his Muslim neighbors—a love born of faith in a power stronger than terrorism. ⟶   —*The Editors*

NEIL SHIGLEY

Invisible People

Why I Make Portraits of San Diego's Homeless

On a cold night in San Diego's Little Italy, I was walking to a gallery opening when I passed a homeless man in a doorway. His eyes caught mine before I could glance away. Inside, as I walked around looking at paintings, the man's face stayed with me. I knew then that I had to do his portrait, and that's how the series "Invisible People" started.

While we're often attracted to images of the rich and famous, too many of us tend to look away from people on the other end of the economic spectrum, the homeless. It's almost second nature for many of us to simply avoid or ignore a homeless person. Often, we act as if the person isn't there. For this reason, these images are presented larger than life. By encountering a face this size, I want each viewer to be confronted by a visible, visceral human being.

What is the difference between the people portrayed here and the rest of us? Not as much as we think. We wake up each day and go to sleep at night. We have hopes and dreams and plans. We want to be respected. We want to be loved.

As I've gotten to know San Diego's homeless men, women, and children, I've come to recognize and admire the incredible character that each of these people possesses, hard earned through years of struggle and survival on the streets. Their nobility, beauty, strength, and vulnerability are plain to see, if only we look rather than turn away.

There are over six thousand homeless people in the San Diego region, and eighteen hundred of them are children. The issue of chronic homelessness is complex, here and elsewhere. I don't pretend to have any answers, but if this work can raise awareness, perhaps we can begin to generate some solutions. If these portraits help to keep even one child from ending up on the streets, then the effort that has gone into making them will be worth it.

Neil Shigley teaches art and illustration at San Diego State University. This article is based on an interview by Maureen Swinger on January 7, 2016. Learn more about the "Invisible People" project at www.neilshigley.com.

Juan 65

Juan, a quiet and dignified man, has been homeless for nineteen years. Originally from Oaxaca, Mexico, Juan has been a field worker most of his life. His hands are solid and tough.

Creating the Portraits

Each portrait starts with a walk through a city, usually San Diego. As I meet people living on the street, I approach them with a great deal of respect. Even though they don't have a home, they still have a space that they call their own. I explain that I am an artist and that I would like to make a portrait. Some say yes, some say no. If they agree, I ask about their life, their history, and their hopes. I take one to two photographs, without trying to pose the subject in any way except to ask if they can face into the light. I am looking for the most honest portrayal I can get, one that touches on the human condition.

From the photo, I create a charcoal drawing. Once I am satisfied with the sketch, I enlarge it to match the size of a piece of Plexiglas. Most are three feet by four feet, but the largest are nine by twelve. I place the drawing behind the Plexiglas and begin to carve with a flexible shaft drill. It takes six to eight hours to carve each sheet. Then I roll the carving with ink, place a piece of paper over it, and rub the surface to transfer the ink onto the paper. When the ink is dry, the paper is soaked in water and then adhered to canvas stretched over a wood panel. At the top of the piece, I write the name and age of each subject, where we met, and the year and number of the print along with my signature. At the bottom of the image, I paint one of the symbols used by drifters during the Great Depression to relay information about a place to other travelers. I try to express the spirit of each encounter with a specific sign, be it a communication of safety, a warning, or a message like "good road to follow."

Ruth 54

I saw Ruth standing on a busy corner near a thrift store, with a sign asking for money. She was squinting into the morning sunlight. Her face was etched with so much tough living. I introduced myself as an artist and asked if she'd let me do her portrait. She agreed, but seemed nervous, so I thanked her again, then took her photo quickly so that she could get back to what she was doing. I learned nothing about her.

Bella 7

While I spoke with her mother, Bella played with her older sister and younger brother. Their happiness was contagious – a stark contrast to their history. Bella's mother grew up homeless. Raised by a gang in Los Angeles, she married early. She told me her husband was very violent, so one night she took the three children and escaped. They found their way to San Diego, where they live on the streets and in shelters.

In the future I plan to create more portraits of women and children who are homeless and unsupported. The children have no say, no choice in regard to their circumstances, and often this life is all they have ever known.

Mark 46

I see Mark often at the freeway off-ramp. He always has a smile and a sign with a positive message. He's trim and handsome and does not do drugs or drink. When he came to see his portrait on display at the gallery, he told me the city had cleared all his stuff that morning, including his tent. That's a big deal for a man who has almost nothing, but he didn't dwell on it. Instead, he reflected on his portrait:

> When I look at the picture, I appreciate what I am, who I am. I like that Neil calls it "Invisible People," 'cause that's who we are. I hold the sign, I don't talk to anyone unless I say hi, and you wouldn't imagine how many brothers have come by me and just cussed me out because they're mad about the way society's going, or maybe I put them in an awkward position: "Now I gotta help him, because he's right there." People can drive by me like a stop sign. Some choose to talk to me, some choose to get out and pray with me. I'd rather be disliked than be ignored. No one wants to be ignored.
>
> So I choose to do what I'm doing now, just living, surviving . . . you can call it surviving. I mean, God feeds rats and roaches; he wouldn't forget me.
>
> The gift that God has for people is something, man. It doesn't have the spark that the devil has with the Jeeps and Range Rovers, and the bars and things like that, but it's beautiful. We're reaching for things that we want, and we never really get what we need. And that's bad. It passes us right by. We have to understand that this is a material world, and everything has a shelf life for a reason; everything will pass. It might take a while for it to pass, but it passes. So it has to be eternal. . . . You got to understand that you're learning something before you go. That saying is a trip, man: "As soon as I died, I started living." It's true. We're learning about somewhere else. It's not over.
>
> And I don't think that God made all of these people down here for us to be separated from each other.

Neil Shigley's interview with Mark appears in full at plough.com/shigley.

Wayne 35

I met Wayne on a sunny day in downtown Los Angeles. I saw him walking – shuffling really. He was slight, missing a shoe, and his clothes didn't fit him very well. When I got closer, I saw that he had an injured foot, so he couldn't put a shoe on it. At first, he seemed shy and reluctant to engage with me. He spoke little English and did not make eye contact. Still, he seemed thankful that someone cared enough to listen. We ended up sitting on the curb and talking for a while. I asked him if I could do his portrait, and he agreed to let me take a photo. I gave him some money for food. He told me that his parents were Italian, that he was thirty-five, and that he had come to LA from Hawaii the previous year. He had a cocaine problem. "I used to be big-time me . . . now I'm sad me," he said. He seemed like a wounded bird – very fragile, quiet, and sad. He told me, "I want Jesus to save me and take me away." ➤

AN INTERVIEW WITH DENISE UWIMANA

Neighbors in Rwanda

Can broken relationships be restored – even
two decades after the genocide?

 N RWANDA IN 1994, in the space of approximately one hundred days from April to mid-July, Hutu militias massacred up to one million or more Tutsis and moderate Hutus, mostly using hand weapons such as machetes, swords, and axes. Often the victims included the killers' longtime neighbors and even friends and relatives. ⟫ Twenty-nine-year-old Denise Uwimana, a Tutsi, was housing seven relatives and friends along with her two sons, aged four and one-and-a-half. Nine months pregnant, she expected her baby's arrival

Previous spread: Villagers, both Tutsi and Hutu, gather to celebrate at the building site of Iriba Shalom International's community center in Mukoma (2015).

any day. Her husband, Charles, was working some thirty-five miles away. On the afternoon of April 16, 1994, militants broke into her home and attacked five inhabitants, leaving them to bleed to death. Remarkably, Denise and her children were spared. Several hours later she went into labor and delivered her third son. ⏩ Denise and her sons survived the genocide against immense odds (a story she tells in a forthcoming book). Many of her relatives, though, were killed. So was her husband – she still does not know how or when his death occurred. ⏩⏩ In spite of this loss, Denise chose to forgive the perpetrators of the genocide and work for reconciliation in her country. She later married Wolfgang Reinhardt, a German theologian and aid coordinator, and founded Iriba Shalom International, a nonprofit organization that provides spiritual and material support to genocide survivors.

PLOUGH: *Denise, choosing the way of reconciliation after what you experienced must have been difficult. Was there anything in your upbringing that prepared you for this?*

DENISE UWIMANA: I was born into a Christian refugee family. In 1962, my parents fled from Rwanda to Burundi, and later to what is now the Democratic Republic of the Congo, because of political unrest caused by radical Hutus who wanted to kill Tutsis. I grew up mostly in the Congo.

As a family, we had a special and treasured tradition: after dinner each night, we would meet and discuss all we had experienced that day. We sang worship songs, my father read a Bible story, and we talked about any misunderstandings that had arisen between us during the day. We forgave one another, exchanged prayer requests, and prayed together. Every morning we children woke up early and ran to our parents' bedroom, where we knelt before their bed, prayed together, and got their blessing for the day.

My parents gave us a solid education in the Christian faith. In my adolescence, I knew what sin was and how to protect myself so as to not be involved in things contrary to my beliefs.

We had a neighbor who loved me and the other village children very much. One day, she became ill with meningitis and was taken to the hospital, where she died one week later. We children were very shocked and cried many tears for her. I started thinking more about the end of life, asking myself where I would go if I would die. While mourning for her, we started meeting in her house for prayer. This prayer meeting grew, and we started confessing our sins and seeking Jesus. It was a kind of revival. Our pastor observed that the number of youth and children meeting together was growing and assigned a church elder to care for us.

Denise, (left) and Charles, (back row third from left) visiting Denise's parents in the Congo in August 1993. This is the only photo Denise has showing her, Charles, and their two young sons (front row).

Had you faced discrimination as a Tutsi before the genocide?

When I was twenty-one years old, friends invited me to visit them in Bugarama, a town in southwest Rwanda. They hoped to help me find a job at CIMERWA, a large cement-manufacturing plant there.

One day, I was walking along the road when the prefect (*préfet*) of the regional authority drove by in his white pickup. He stopped his car and arrested me on the pretext that I didn't have the correct papers. When he searched my handbag and found a photograph of a friend who had invited me to apply for a job at CIMERWA, he accused me of coming to spy on the company. He took me to the mayor, hoping to convince him to send me to a nearby prison, but he would not.

Dissatisfied, the prefect then took me to an immigration office near the border. He told the Rwandan officials there that I was a refugee Tutsi from the Congo seeking employment in Rwanda. He knew that I had become friends with Charles, the man I later married, and he knew that Charles was helping me find a job at CIMERWA. After some discussion, they decided not to send me to prison but instead to fine me and expel me from Rwanda. On the receipt for the fine, the prefect stated the official reason for my punishment was that I was *inzererezi*, a Rwandan term for a vagrant woman or lowlife. The officials heaped verbal abuse on me. The next day, the prefect followed me to the Congo border crossing. "You will never get a job in Rwanda. There is no chance for Tutsis in Rwanda," he shouted after me.

This experience made me hate Rwanda. I did not want to hear anything more about the country. If my housemate tuned the radio to Rwandan news or music, I turned it off. Every time I looked at the receipt for the fine, I got into a rage, and fear and hatred toward Hutus rose up in my heart. I suffered from nightmares. My family realized that I was deeply affected. "That evil man, the prefect, broke her heart," they said.

> ≫ **Luitpolt told me that because he had found the cross, he never wanted to betray Jesus again.** ≪

I kept praying that God would heal my wounds and help me to forgive. One day, as I was staring yet again at the receipt from the prefect, an inner voice seemed to say, "As long as you keep that piece of paper, you will never forgive him. You should get rid of it." I tore up the receipt and forgave the prefect and the immigration officials. After some months, I got a letter from friends in Rwanda telling me that the prefect regretted his unjust behavior toward me, admitted I was innocent, and asked them to find me and apologize on his behalf. He even met Charles and reconciled with him. In the end, I did get a job with CIMERWA and moved back to Rwanda.

In the months before April 1994, were there warning signs that something like the genocide might be coming?

As has occurred before other genocides, the media carried out a contemptuous propaganda campaign. Already in 1990, the *Kangura* newspaper published "The Ten Commandments of the Hutu" which denounced every Hutu who married a Tutsi woman as a traitor, branded Tutsis as being dishonest in business dealings, demanded Hutu dominance of higher education, and required that only Hutus should hold strategically important offices or serve in the Rwandan armed forces. Most inhuman was the eighth of these commandments, which stated, "Hutus must cease to have pity for the Tutsi." The radio station RTLM incessantly broadcasted the message that Tutsis are cockroaches and snakes; this station later orchestrated the massacres. Once a group of people is dehumanized in this way, it becomes easy to kill them.

Rwanda is the African country with the largest percentage of Christians. How does that fact square with genocide?

Long before the genocide, Rwanda's church leaders were mostly silent toward or supportive of the ideology of Hutu superiority. Members of all churches spread divisive propaganda and were even actively involved in the killings. When a cardinal from Rome visited Rwanda, he asked the church leaders he was meeting with, "Are you saying that the blood of tribalism is deeper than the waters of baptism?" One leader answered, "Yes it is."

Sadly, Christian education in Rwanda did not teach a mature and critical attitude to government based on the standards of the gospel, but rather emphasized blind obedience toward those in power. Whatever the leaders in power commanded was supposed to be carried out. There was no tradition of Christian resistance, even if the powers of state and church demanded something completely contrary to the will of God as shown in the Bible.

In your own Pentecostal denomination, several members committed crimes during the genocide. What was your response?

I was disappointed in my church, and very angry. This issue has not gone away. Just

Luitpolt and Josephine

recently, in early January 2016, we heard about a pastor from our church who was sentenced to life in prison because of his involvement in the killings.

Despite this, in the months after the genocide, an inner voice told me, "The devil is everywhere. Stay here in this church. Help this people to change. You will be a light for them." After the genocide, many left their churches, but I stayed in mine and am still a member today.

In 1994, did you know any Hutu Christians who stood up for you?

Yes, an exceptional Hutu couple, Luitpolt and Josephine, showed me what it means to love your neighbor in a time of genocide. Luitpolt worked as a car mechanic at CIMERWA, the factory where I was also employed. He met me secretly almost every day to pass on messages of encouragement: "Stay strong." "Do not be afraid." "We stand with you."

Josephine took my baby son to the clinic for his vaccinations because it was too dangerous for me to go. On the way, she came to a militia checkpoint. She said, "I am not prepared to let this child be killed. If you want to kill him, first kill me." She was pregnant at that time and later gave birth to a baby girl whom she named Sauvée, or Rescued One.

After the genocide, I was able to meet with them and ask why they were willing to die while other Hutus were proud to exterminate Tutsis. Luitpolt told me that once soldiers had grabbed him and pushed him on the ground to kill him. He had told them, "I am ready to die. Tutsis whom you kill are also human beings and bleed like me." He was not a pastor or a priest; he was not a church leader. But he told me that because he had been saved and found the cross, he never wanted to betray Jesus again. That is why he and Josephine did what they could and suffered with me in my darkest hours.

After 1994, you started visiting former neighbors regardless of their ethnic classification. How did that come about?

When I came back to my village after the genocide, some residents welcomed me, but most kept a distance. Of course, I was deeply wounded inside. I had no hope and didn't care about keeping up friendships. I would just attend church and then come straight home.

Before the genocide, though, I had been visiting poor and sick people on behalf of my church, bringing them food and encouragement. After I came back to my village, I gradually began doing this again. My visits seemed like a miracle to my neighbors because they saw that I made the first move. They felt guilty and thought I would never come; even if they were not actively involved, they were Hutu and I was a survivor. They would ask, "How is it that you can come to see us?"

> ## » The militia member raised his sword, ready to kill my sons and me, but he did not. «

You started a nonprofit organization, Iriba Shalom International, to help genocide survivors. What inspired this decision?

During the genocide I made a vow that if I survived, I would use my life to tell people that God exists and to encourage them to believe in him.

A few years after the genocide, I gave up my job at CIMERWA and started working for a Christian organization called Solace Ministries, because I realized there were many widows and orphans who needed help. We would visit them or gather them together to hear their stories, and we'd look for ways to help them heal and get back to normal life.

One of the places I visited was Mukoma, a village in the same county as Bugarama, the town where I survived. I went there because my mother-in-law, Consoletia, lives there. While I was in Mukoma, some widows came to see me and told me their stories. On April 14, 1994, a group of murderers who had already killed these women's husbands and older sons forced them to bring their baby boys as well. The women had to lay their babies on a big log, where the killers cut off each baby's head with a machete.

These women's plight touched me very deeply. Mukoma hadn't received any help because it was so remote; our organization usually only worked in cities or larger towns. But when I heard their story, I realized that it was connected to my own.

After the birth of my third son on April 17, 1994, I had been taken to CIMERWA's small clinic. Shortly after I arrived, a man had walked in bragging, "Do you know what we did in Mukoma? We killed all their boys!" Now I suddenly realized that this murderer had first been in Mukoma and then had come to the clinic intending to do the same to us. He raised his sword, ready to kill my sons and me, but he did not. This miracle was one of the reasons I founded Iriba Shalom, which is based in Mukoma.

One of Iriba Shalom's programs aims to connect survivors with sponsors in Western countries. It's helpful for survivors to know that there are people in the wider world who care about them and their stories. Iriba Shalom is also in the process of building a community center in Mukoma to provide a safe location for trauma counseling, fellowship, medical assistance, and practical help related to finances and the daily challenges of widows' lives.

Denise, (right) visiting the home of a genocide widow in Mukoma to hear her story

Is Rwanda as a country finding healing from its past?

Reconciliation is the official policy in Rwanda today. It is a good policy, but obviously reconciliation cannot simply be ordered from above. It is always a miracle when somebody can forgive those who tortured and killed his or her loved ones. In Rwanda this miracle is happening on such a great scale that even secular observers are astonished. As a friend of mine said, "We cannot overestimate the power of the cross in reconciliation."

Truth and confession are important to the healing process. Not all churches have publicly confessed their involvement in the genocide. But many have, and are now playing an active role in the healing of society. According to Professor Vincent Sezibera, a leading Rwandan trauma expert, the most effective healing from trauma happens in a community-based approach as in the fellowship of Iriba Shalom. When survivors help each other – when they pray, sing, dance, eat, and work together in a loving community – they feel a new sense of purpose and dignity. The same is true when they receive support through sponsorship or a local "alternative family," and when they learn how to generate an income.

We've seen several examples of survivors now working together with those who murdered their neighbors or family members. At an Iriba Shalom event, one woman said of the young killer of her children, "He's like my son now." He added, "She is my mother, and I help her as much as I can." ⤳

Interview by Erna Albertz for Plough *on January 12, 2016. To read the testimony of Drocella Nduwimana, another survivor, see* plough.com/rwandasurvivor.

Aristarkh Lentulov, *Churches, New Jerusalem,* 1917

Did the Early Christians
Understand Jesus?

GERHARD LOHFINK

Nonviolence, Love of Neighbor, and Imminent Expectation

There are statements

so bewildering that they are quoted again and again. Among these is a remark, now a century old, by the French biblical scholar Alfred Loisy: "Jesus proclaimed the kingdom of God – and what came was the church."[1] I'll leave to the side the question of what Loisy himself meant by this sentence. Rather, I'll focus on how it's understood by those who gleefully quote it. Usually, they understand it as bitterly ironic.

Gerhard Lohfink, a Catholic priest, was professor of New Testament studies at the University of Tübingen. Since 1986, he has been a member of the Catholic Integrated Community and lives in Bad Tölz, Germany. This is a translation from German of his talk on November 21, 2015 at a conference commemorating Eberhard Arnold (see overleaf).

Here, on the one side, is the kingdom of God that Jesus proclaimed: the immense, all-comprehensive, yet incomprehensible transformation of the world under God's reign – and there, on the other side, is the church that came after Easter: a finite body with all the limitations of any other social structure. Clearly, then, there's a gaping chasm between Jesus' proclamation and the post-Easter reality! Here the glory of the kingdom of God; there the bitter paltriness of the actual existing church.

I'll say immediately what merit I find in this approach: None. None at all. For it rends open a cleft between the will of Jesus and the reality of the church in a way that does injustice to both Jesus and the church. How so?

First of all, because it was Jesus himself who characterized the onset of the kingdom as small and utterly inconspicuous. Think of his images of the mustard seed (Mark 4:30–32), of the yeast (Matt. 13:33), of the endangered seed (Mark 4:1–9), or of the seed that grows in secret (Mark 4:26–29).

Second, because the kingdom as proclaimed by Jesus never lies removed from society. Repeatedly, of course, people have attempted to turn it into that, seeking to project the kingdom into the far-off future, or into absolute transcendence, or into the depths of the human soul. But for Jesus, the kingdom of God is a concrete social reality. God's *basileia* (kingly rule) has its starting point in a real people. The transformation of the world through the reign of God must begin in Israel.

To be sure, the kingdom of God and the people of God are not identical. But they are strongly connected. In the Lord's Prayer, Jesus tells us to ask for the coming of the kingdom. But just before, he has us pray for the gathering and sanctification of the people of God. That is what is meant by the words, "Hallowed be your name."[2] Behind this request is the theology of the book of Ezekiel.[3]

---

[1] Alfred Loisy, *L'Évangile et l'Église*, 2nd ed. (Bellevue, 1903), 155.

[2] G. Lohfink, *Das Vaterunser neu ausgelegt* (Verlag Katholisches Bibelwerk, 2013), 51–59.

[3] E.g., Ezek. 20:22, 41, 55; 36:22–28.

Jesus proclaims the kingdom of God and announces its coming. Even more, he initiates, right in the midst of Israel, the practical transformation of the world that God's reign signifies. His announcement of God's kingdom is connected to the gathering of Israel.[4]

Since the church is nothing other than the Israel that listens to, follows after, and is made holy by Jesus, the kingdom and the church are very closely connected. The fact that Jesus proclaimed the kingdom, and what came after Easter was the church is no tragic fall, no bitter irony of history, no perversion of Jesus' will; rather, it follows directly from the social dimension of Jesus' kingdom proclamation.

Against this background I would like to explore whether the early church understood what Jesus wanted and whether it lived it out. I realize, of course, that such a broad subject actually demands far more space. From among the many possible approaches, I will examine three sample topics: (1) nonviolence, (2) love of neighbor, and (3) the imminent expectation of the end of the age. In each case, I will give my reasons for selecting that particular topic.

Nonviolence

In recent decades, Islam has been gaining strength all over the world, showing a new self-confidence. No objections there. Unfortunately, however, within the broad terrain of Islam we see terrorist Islamist movements emerging ever more powerfully – groups that view murder as a service to God.[5]

For people shaped by Enlightenment values, such inhuman violence only reinforces a preexisting antipathy to religion. This antipathy encompasses Christianity (and Israel) as well. More and more often, one hears the claim that all monotheistic religions, by their very nature, harbor a deeply rooted urge toward violence. Israel, the church, and Islam are then all mentioned in the same breath.

Participants gather in Fulda's Michaelskirche, a ninth-century church where Eberhard Arnold went to pray for guidance in facing Nazi persecution.

Photograph by Wolfgang Krauss

Can we live out the Sermon on the Mount?

To seek an answer to this question, in November 2015 over a hundred people from Europe, Africa, and North America – students, farmers, peace activists, members of Catholic, Protestant, and Anabaptist communities – gathered in Fulda, Germany. Titled *Bergpredigt leben* ("Living the Sermon on the Mount"), the event was organized by Plough and the Fellowship of Reconciliation in Germany to mark the eightieth anniversary of the death of Eberhard Arnold (1883–1935), founder of the Bruderhof and founding editor of Plough. Professor Gerhard Lohfink gave the keynote address, which appears here in an abridged English translation. Watch his talk and other presentations at *plough.com/fuldaevent*. ➘

Against this claim, we must emphatically repeat: already the Israel of the Old Testament, in its crowning texts, renounced every form of violence. The radical nonviolence of Jesus has its roots in the Old Testament, above all in the theology of the Suffering Servant found in Isaiah, chapters 40–55. The Suffering Servant stands for deported Israel in exile in Babylon. Israel, the Suffering Servant, will not cry or lift up his voice. He looks to God alone to justify him in the face of the injustice he endures. He gives his back to those who strike him. And he does not open his mouth, like a lamb that is led to the slaughter (Isa. 42:2; 49:4; 50:6; 53:7).

The so-called Servant Songs in Isaiah speak of a beaten, kidnapped, enslaved Israel who looks to God alone and who – precisely through his absolute rejection of violence – becomes salvation for the Gentile nations.[6]

Take note: the Book of Isaiah is also the book that introduced pure monotheism in Israel, sweeping away Israel's earlier worldview in which the exclusive worship of YHWH coexisted with the belief that other gods existed as well. Thus, at the precise time and place at which monotheism prevails in Israel, we find emerging in the people of God the most explicit texts about radical nonviolence. Conclusion: Those who wish to link violence to monotheism are free to peruse the Quran. But they should keep their hands off the monotheism of the Bible, otherwise they will only prove their ignorance.

In our gathering today, as we commemorate the eightieth anniversary of Eberhard Arnold's death, I think it right and fitting that the theme of nonviolence takes first place in my lecture. Eberhard Arnold not only loved the Sermon on the Mount: it gripped him. Here I must refrain from listing individually all the places in the Sermon on the Mount where Jesus calls for nonviolence.[7] Instead, I will make the following three points:

(1) The Sermon on the Mount is addressed to Jesus' disciples and, through them, to all Israel as the people of God. Jesus' summons to nonviolence is not a manifesto for the state. The state cannot give to everyone who asks. The state cannot turn the other cheek, nor can it apply to itself the sentence, "Do not resist an evildoer" (Matt. 5:39). The Sermon on the Mount is meant for a people of God that lives out, as a nation among the nations, the kingdom way of life taught by Jesus. By so doing, the people of God is to be a sign of peace for the nations.

(2) In his demands for nonviolence, Jesus speaks, as he does in many other places, with the provocative exaggeration of a prophet. That doesn't change the fact that he is addressing real-life ways of behaving – his words really are to be lived out and used as models to illuminate analogous situations. Jesus really does forbid his disciples to use violence, and he is convinced that anyone who accepts his word can live without defensive violence and without retaliation.

> Already the Old Testament, in its crowning texts, renounced every form of violence.

---

[4] G. Lohfink, *Jesus of Nazareth* (Liturgical Press, 2012), 39–58.

[5] C. W. Troll, "Quran, Gewalt, Theologie," *Christ in der Gegenwart*, no. 43, (2014) 485–486.

[6] G. Lohfink and L. Weimer, *Maria – nicht ohne Israel* (Herder, 2012), 223–229.

[7] G. Lohfink, *Wem gilt die Bergpredigt?* (Herder, 1988), 42–45.

Aristarkh
Lentulov,
Gursuf, 1913

(3) Jesus' demands for nonviolence are not restricted to the Sermon on the Mount. They form the backdrop as well to the major Mission Discourse found in Mark 6, Matthew 10, and Luke 9–10. When Jesus commissions his disciples to travel throughout Israel proclaiming everywhere the kingdom of God, he forbids them to wear sandals (Luke 10:4), carry a staff (Luke 9:3), or take money in their pocket (Luke 10:4). He tells them not even to take bread with them (Mark 6:8).

The intention here is not to imitate the kind of self-abnegation for which itinerant Cynic philosophers were then known. Rather, the disciples' lack of resources is meant as a sign separating them from the belligerence of the anti-Roman resistance fighters. Someone without a staff cannot defend himself; someone without shoes on his feet is unable, on Palestine's rocky terrain, even to run away. Someone who carries no money is utterly destitute, helpless, and dependent on sympathizers within the Jesus movement. For Jesus, this immediately recognizable contrast from the holy warriors of his time had fundamental importance. The Jesus movement was not to be confused with the militant Zealots.

Did the early church grasp and live out the same radical nonviolence that for Jesus was a sign of the coming reign of God?

In what follows, I do not seek to paint a romantic, glorified picture of a flawless and heroic early Christianity. Even at that time, the church contained shocking wretchedness, woeful cowardice, and heavy guilt. Nevertheless, since nowadays it is Christian criminality that gets the most attention, we must speak about the other side: the early church's faithfulness to the gospel. What's more, we must examine not only what the Christians *were*, but also what they *wanted to be*.

What matters for the questions before us is not only the degree of success in realizing Jesus' teaching, but also the mode of consciousness that shapes behavior. Did the Sermon on the Mount form part of the early church's consciousness? Was there a living awareness of Jesus' demand for nonviolence?

If we phrase the question in that way, we stumble on a fascinating phenomenon. The Book of Isaiah, chapter 2, describes how one day the Gentile nations would come to Mount Zion.[8] They would come to leave behind their desperation, their existential fear, and the horrors of their incessant wars. They would come to learn from Israel – above all, to learn how these devastating wars could be ended. For from Zion goes forth the decisive, enlightening word of God. This is the context for the famous words: "They [the Gentile nations] shall beat their swords into plowshares, and their spears into pruning hooks; nation shall not lift up sword against nation, neither shall they learn war anymore" (Isa. 2:4).

The theologians of the early church understood this prophetic word to refer to the Gentile church.[9] They said: Mount Zion is the church. From there the word of Jesus goes forth. We, as Gentile Christians, are making our way to the true God. When we were baptized, we learned to lay down our weapons; we turned our swords and spears into tools for peace. We are no longer learning war. Isaiah 2 has been fulfilled; the prophecy has become reality. We no longer use violence.

It would be gratifying if what the theologians wrote was actually lived out in Christian communities. Here is where we can draw on the so-called apologists.[10]

The apologists, several of whom had been pagan philosophers before becoming Christians, wrote defenses of the life of the Christians. Because Christians refused to participate in many pagan traditions and practices, they were accused of "hatred of humanity" and of all kinds of depravity.[11] In response, the apologists described the actual life of their fellow believers. Running throughout their writings is an enormous, unshakable confidence that Christian praxis has a persuasive power in and of itself. Repeatedly the apologists tell their pagan readers: not only do we have the true philosophy, but we also have the right practice, and both are closely connected. For example, Athenagoras of Athens writes in his *Legatio* (AD 177):

> Among us, you will find uneducated persons, and artisans, and old women, who, even if they cannot prove the benefit of [our faith] through words, through their

> When we were baptized, we learned to lay down our weapons. The prophecy of Isaiah has become reality.

---

[8] See M. P. Maier, *Völkerwallfahrt im Jesaja-Buch* (Walter de Gruyter, 2015).

[9] Lohfink, *Wem gilt die Bergpredigt?*, 161–192.

[10] Sources in G. Lohfink, *Wie hat Jesus Gemeinde gewollt?*, rev. ed. (Verlag Katholisches Bibelwerk, 2015), part 4.

[11] E.g., Tacitus, *Annals*, XV 44:2–5.

deeds they prove the benefit that results from our devotion [or faith]; for they do not memorize speeches, but rather they exhibit good works; when struck, they do not strike back, and when they are robbed, they do not bring charges; to everyone who asks of them, they give, and they love their neighbors as themselves.[12]

Here Athenagoras quotes the Sermon on the Mount directly. Many other early Christian apologists argue similarly, though I must refrain here from citing them all. But one thing seems obvious to me: A document written to defend the Christian faith needed to be based on the actual way that the Christians lived. Otherwise it would be nothing but empty words.

An important related question remains: What was the early church's attitude to war? Did the bishops forbid believers to serve in the Roman army? That is a test that would clarify a great deal. However, the current state of research is complex.[13] Many baptized Christians became soldiers, and many soldiers were baptized. As a historic fact, this must be regarded as settled and well verified.[14] Also, in the early church there was no universal principle of Christian pacifism.[15] (Naturally one can hardly expect that, for as we have already seen, the Sermon on the Mount does not regulate public life but rather the life of Jesus' disciples among themselves.)

> We Christians are all priests, since we sanctify the society in which we live.

On the other hand, there were theologians in the early church who opposed military service by Christians.[16] The most important of these is Origen. Celsus, an opponent of the Christians, had penned an attack accusing them of failing to help uphold the state; he charged that they instead distanced themselves from Roman society. When war had to be waged against the barbarians violating the borders of the empire, wrote Celsus, the Christians would leave the emperor in the lurch.

Origen answers these charges in *Contra Celsum*, a text written in AD 248, arguing: You pagans do not require your priests to do military service. By the same token, we Christians are all priests, since we sanctify the society in which we live. We pray for the emperor. We pray that right will prevail and that only just wars will be fought. It is far more important for us to do that than to take part in war.[17]

In this text, we find a very clearly defined position on the question of whether a Christian can be a soldier, as well as an acute awareness of the church's principal task in society: that is, to preserve pagan society from destroying itself in wars waged out of greed and lust for conquest. Here we come very close to Jesus' understanding of what the people of God should be: yeast within society – and that thanks to their nonviolence.

The theologians are hardly our only sources in regard to military service. At least one church order discusses this whole question as a matter of canon law,[18] the *Apostolic Tradition* attributed to Hippolytus (ca. AD 150–235):

A soldier in command[19] must be told not to kill people; if he is ordered so to do, he shall not carry it out. Nor should he take the [military] oath. If he will not agree, let him cease or be cast out [as a baptismal candidate]. Anyone who has the power of the sword, or who is a civil magistrate wearing the purple either let him cease or be cast out [as a baptismal candidate]. If a [baptismal] candidate or a believer wishes to become a soldier, let them be cast out, for they have despised God.[20]

I must emphasize: this church order never applied to the whole church. All the same, it shows that Jesus' rejection of violence had not completely disappeared from Christians' consciousness, including in regard to military service. Although the *Apostolic Tradition* takes the existence of Christian soldiers as a given, it still insists that one who has become a catechumen (baptismal candidate) may no longer sign up as a soldier.

Love of Neighbor

The topic of love for neighbor is widely misunderstood. Nowadays we're constantly being told, "You can only love others if you first love yourself." This mantra isn't just repeated by psychologists and psychotherapists; it's also become the dominant theme of twenty-first century devotional literature.

And it is not completely wrong. Yet the commandment to love others "as you love yourself" cannot be trotted out as a reason to embrace self-love and self-acceptance. Love of neighbor in the Bible is never based on self-acceptance. The Bible does not speak a word about self-acceptance; it speaks of repentance. It also doesn't speak a word about reconciling with oneself, but rather of reconciling with God and with one's neighbor.

In the Bible, the command "Love your neighbor as you love yourself" does not refer to the individual "I" in the modern sense. Rather, the "I" here means one's family. This observation is illustrated beautifully in the account of the calling of Abraham. God says to Abraham: "I will make of you a great nation, and I will bless you, and make your name great, so that you will be a blessing" (Gen 12:2).

> The Bible does not speak a word about self-acceptance; it speaks of repentance.

---

[12] Athenagoras, *Legatio* 11, trans. George Kalantzis.

[13] Sources: A. v. Harnack, *Militia Christi* (Tübingen, 1905; Darmstadt, 1963); H. v. Campenhausen, "Der Kriegsdienst der Christen in der Kirche des Altertums," *Universitas* 12 (1957), 1147–1156; H. Karpp, "Die Stellung der Alten Kirche zu Kriegsdienst und Krieg," *Evangelische Theologie* 17 (1957), 496–515. Especially: H. C. Brennecke, "'An fidelis ad militiam converti possit?': Frühchristliches Bekenntnis und Militärdienst im Widerspruch?", *Die Weltlichkeit des Glaubens in der Alten Kirche,* ed. D. Wyrwa (De Gruyter, 1997), 45–100.

[14] Tertullian, *De corona* 1 (*solus fortis inter tot fratres commilitones*), 42–43; Tertullian, *Apology* 5,6; 37,4; 42,3; Eusebius, *Church History* VI 41:22–23; VII 11:20; VII 15–16; VIII 1:7.

[15] Campenhausen, "Kriegsdienst," 1148: "Not one single church father expressed doubts that in the world as it is, wars must be fought, and they therefore found no reason to single out the military profession for condemnation."

[16] Apart from Origen, see Tertullian, *De corona und De idololatria* 19; see also Lactantius, *Institutiones divinae* VI 20,15–17. Thus the discussion of whether a Christian may be a soldier first starts in the third century.

[17] Origen, *Contra Celsum* VIII 68.73.75.

[18] By contrast, the canons of Elvira are silent on the question of military service by Christians, although they address in detail questions of Christian life amid pagan society. See Brennecke, "Frühchristliches Bekenntnis," 93.

[19] In the Roman empire, civil and military authority were not separated. The term *militia* can mean either. *Miles* normally refers to a soldier, but can also refer to an armed imperial official.

[20] Hippolytus, *On the Apostolic Tradition*, trans. Alistair Stewart-Sykes.

Who does this "you" refer to? Abraham of course. But not Abraham alone. For not only he but also his wife Sarai, his nephew Lot, and the persons they had acquired in Haran all left their old homeland (Gen. 12:4–5). That is, Abraham set out with his whole extended family, with his cattle and tents, toward Canaan.

This linguistic background, which in the Old Testament is self-evident, is the setting for the commandment of neighbor-love in Leviticus 19:18, 34. Accordingly, here "Love your neighbor as yourself" means: The help and solidarity that everyone in Israel owes his own relatives, especially his direct family, should be extended to all Israelites. The boundaries of one's own family should be broken through so as to include the whole people of God as brothers and sisters – including strangers, and even those whom one's family and relatives consider enemies. That is what Leviticus 19 is saying. This thought is light years away from the individualistic self-love so widely advocated today.

> **For the early Christians, love of neighbor meant practical mutual care.**

It is just this revolutionary move that Jesus picks up on. He goes on to radicalize it further. In the Pentateuch the commandment to love God and the commandment to love one's neighbor are unconnected: one is found in Deuteronomy 6, the other in Leviticus 19. Jesus combines the two,[21] and what is more, he makes the command to love one's neighbor equal in importance to the command to love God (Matt. 22:37–40). For him, these two commandments cannot be separated. He places both together at the center of the Torah.

According to Jesus, those whom we are to love are not distant; we are not told to embrace all humankind as our neighbors "in spirit." No, our task is more concrete: to put aside enmities within the people of God, to treat even strangers living within this people as brothers and sisters – that is, to accept them into the protected space of mutual respect and solidarity. This is the biblical meaning of *agapē*.

Did the early church understand and live out this radical love of neighbor in the way Jesus did – as a sign of the approaching reign of God?

It would certainly be fruitful at this point to make a thorough study of Paul's letters. They make clear how for him, *agapē* within the church was central. Paul's letters also show that for him, just as in the Old Testament, *agapē* consisted not of beautiful feelings but rather of mutual acceptance, respect, help, and solidarity. For Paul this solidarity extended even beyond the Christian church. In that case, however, he no longer speaks of *agapē* but rather of "doing good."[22] Finally, Paul's letters show that Christian *agapē* has its deepest root in Jesus, who gave himself on the cross.

I will not delve more deeply here into Paul's letters, but rather will turn at this point to the early church of the second and third centuries. Did this church live out the mutual *agapē* that was at the heart of Jesus' kingdom praxis? Here much evidence could be adduced from both the early Christian theologians and the early apologists. I have chosen to focus on three Christian texts.

The first is an important passage from Justin's *Apology,* written around AD 150–155. Chapter 67 of the *Apology* is noteworthy because it is the oldest description

Aristarkh Lentulov, *Night on Patriarch Ponds,* 1928

we have of the church's celebration of the Eucharist, including the collection at the end of the service:

> And they who are well-to-do, and willing, give what each thinks fit; and what is collected is deposited with the president, who succors the orphans and widows and those who, through sickness or any other cause, are in want, and those who are in bonds and the strangers sojourning among us.[23]

The Sunday collection, then, benefited all those in the church who needed help. Thus a social safety net came into being that was unique in antiquity. It was based on mutual help and voluntary contributions collected at the celebration of the Lord's Supper. When the early Christians spoke of *agapē*, love of neighbor, what they meant was this mutual care.

Love of neighbor, then, was no empty phrase. *Agapē* proved itself as a practical way of addressing economic and social needs within the church. This does not mean, of course, that it was limited to economic need. In the year 260, when the

---

[21] No ancient Jewish texts juxtapose love of God and love of neighbor as Jesus did, thus connecting them and making them central to the Torah. The text that comes closest is "Testaments of the Twelve Patriarchs," although it is disputed whether these are Jewish-Christian writings or a Jewish base text with Christian interpolations. For the juxtaposition of love of God and love of neighbor in ancient Judaism, see A. Nissen, *Gott und der Nächste im antiken Judentum* (Mohr, 1974), esp. 230–244. Nissen notes, "Nowhere in all of ancient Jewish literature prior to the Middle Ages do we find a Deut. 6:5 and Lev. 19:18 connected together" (241, n642).

[22] E.g., 1 Thess. 5:15; Gal. 6:9–10; 1 Pet. 2:17.

[23] Justin, *First Apology* 67; trans. Robertson-Donaldson.

plague was raging in the metropolis of Alexandria, the local bishop Dionysius wrote in a letter:

> The most of our brethren were unsparing in their exceeding love and brotherly kindness. They held fast to each other and visited the sick fearlessly, and ministered to them continually, serving them in Christ. And they died with them most joyfully, taking the affliction of others, and drawing the sickness from their neighbors to themselves and willingly receiving their pains. . . .

> But with the heathen everything was quite otherwise. They deserted those who began to be sick, and fled from their dearest friends. And they cast them out into the streets when they were half dead, and left the dead like refuse, unburied.[24]

Even those inclined to dismiss such texts as over-generalizations must still admit: here is at the very least a description of how the Christians saw themselves and of how they wanted to be.

Until now I have based my argument on Christian sources. Now I would like to cite at least one pagan source – and it is not the only one that could be cited. The Roman emperor Julian, a firm opponent of Christianity, writes in the year 362 to Arsakios, the heathen high priest of Galatia:

> Atheism [i.e., the Christian faith!] has been specially advanced through the loving service rendered to strangers, and through their care for the burial of the dead. It is a scandal that there is not a single Jew who is a beggar, and that the godless Galileans care not only for their own poor but for ours as well; while those who belong to us look in vain for the help that we should render them.[25]

And in a similar programmatic letter to Theodoros, the high priest of the province of Asia, Emperor Julian writes:

> I am of the opinion that, because it has reached a point that the poor are ignored and neglected by our priests, the godless Galileans, who noticed this, have resorted to this practice of philanthropy.[26]

Even though Julian accuses the Christians of ulterior motives in their practice of *agapē*, his letter indicates that the apologists were evidently writing factually: the church's social system functioned so well that it supported even non-Christians. This solidarity must have made a deep impression on outsiders; it was one of the reasons for the rapid spread of Christianity.

Imminent Expectation

Jesus proclaimed the kingdom of God, the reign of God. In itself, this would have been nothing new. Many people in Israel believed in God's reign. And many Jewish groups of Jesus' time hoped that this reign would soon be revealed and that, in the near future, it would arrive and triumph.

Aristarkh Lentulov, *The Belfry of Ivan the Great,* 1915

What was unique with Jesus was that the kingdom of God he proclaimed was coming – not just soon or in the near future – but now. Jesus said: in the mighty deeds that I am doing in the power of God, the kingdom is already here (Luke 11:20; 17:21). Already now it is transforming the people of God unstoppably, step by step, and through the people of God, it is transforming the world.

The kingdom is so near that Jesus' hearers need to repent now. There is no longer any time for postponing repentance. Now, today, Jesus' hearers need to decide to accept the kingdom in faith and to become active in its power. They need to make a decision.

Once again, then, I pose the question: Did the early church follow Jesus in this matter as well? Were they faithful to him here too?

This question cannot be asked superficially. That is, we should not ask: Did the early church adopt and preserve the schema of imminence in time? Instead we should ask: Did the early church understand, adopt, and live out the heart of what was meant by imminent expectation? Did it grasp the presence of the kingdom? Did it grasp that the decisive thing is already happening – that liberation and salvation are already here? And did it grasp the urgent nearness of the kingdom, which leaves no time to postpone repentance?

---

[24] Eusebius, *Church History VII,* 22:7–10; trans. Robertson-Donaldson.

[25] Julian, Epistola Nr. 39, in B. K. Weis, *Julian: Briefe* (Heimeran: 1973).

[26] Julian, Epistola 48, 305 C.

Aristarkh
Lentulov,
Moscow, 1913

The only possible answer is yes. To be sure, for a while the early church retained the concept of imminence in time. But at the same time it was already in the process of reconstructing it. The church spoke less and less of the kingdom of God or of its imminence *in terms of time*. Something else took the place of these concepts.

That something is the early church's declaration that the Spirit is present. The Holy Spirit is the inauguration of the last days (Acts 2:14–21). It is the advance guarantee of the coming fulfillment. Through the Holy Spirit, the world is being newly created in preparation for this fulfillment.[27] Through the Holy Spirit, the Risen One is a constant presence, filling the church with the power of his resurrection (Rom. 8:9–11). Thus the early church's theology of the Spirit is both the equivalent and the exact continuation of Jesus' proclamation of the kingdom of God.

Just as Jesus' proclamation of the kingdom of God was accompanied by symbolic acts – his mighty deeds, after all, were symbols of the breaking in of God's reign – so also the church's receiving of the Spirit is accompanied by tangible signs: the sacraments. The sacraments are symbolic eschatological acts.

This is evident in the Lord's Supper. Its hallmark, the early church's cry "Come, Lord Jesus"[28] is still heard in churches today when the congregation prays, "We proclaim your death, O Lord, and profess your resurrection, until you come again."

The same is true of baptism. It is an eschatological sign, a sealing for the end of the age – and yet at the same time this sacrament obligates us to begin a new life in the present world. Whoever has died with Christ in baptism is born into the new society of the church.

The sacrament of reconciliation, too, is an eschatological sacrament. By confessing our guilt before the church, we come before the seat of God's final judgment. The verdict of the church anticipates and stands for the verdict of the Last Judgment – and does so as a word of forgiveness and reconciliation.

The sacraments contain eschatological dynamite – and they are the place in which the church has lived out and does live out Jesus' eschatology of the now.

I will close with a single text. It comes from the great theologian and bishop Cyprian, who shortly before, probably in the year 245, had received baptism. This had transformed him. In a self-portrait that anticipates Augustine's *Confessions*, Cyprian hints at the uncertainties of his earlier life – the dark aspects, the wrong paths, the moral aberrations, the hardness of heart, the deeply rooted sins, the despair. Cyprian says he had thought it impossible to divest himself of the old man.

> But after [baptism], when the stain of my past life had been washed away by the aid of the water of regeneration, a light from above poured itself upon my chastened and pure heart; afterwards when I had drunk of the Spirit from heaven a second birth restored me into a new man; immediately, in a marvelous manner, doubtful matters clarified themselves, the closed opened, the shadowy shone with light, what seemed impossible was able to be accomplished, so that it was possible to acknowledge that what formerly was born of the flesh and lived submissive to sins was earthly, and what the Holy Spirit already was animating began to be of God.[29]

Cyprian describes his baptism entirely with words drawn from Scripture. But his own experience, that of a man for whom everything has been turned upside-down, grips and permeates the text. Something similar must have happened to countless other Christians. There is no other way to explain how so many found the courage to face persecution and martyrdom by imperial officials. Cyprian, too, died a martyr. During the Valerian persecution, on September 14, 248, he was beheaded near Carthage.

By receiving the Spirit in baptism, the Christians of the early church experienced the power of God's reign. They knew that with baptism, a new life had begun for them. From then on, they lived in the today of the kingdom of God. ⇘

Translated from German by Emmy Barth Maendel and Peter Mommsen.

[27] Matt. 12:28; Rom. 8:18–30; 2 Cor. 1:22; 5:5; Heb. 6:4–5.
[28] 1 Cor. 16:22; Rev. 22:20; *Didache* 10:6.
[29] *Ad Donatum* 4; trans. Roy Deferrari.

By receiving the Spirit in baptism, the early Christians experienced the power of God's reign.

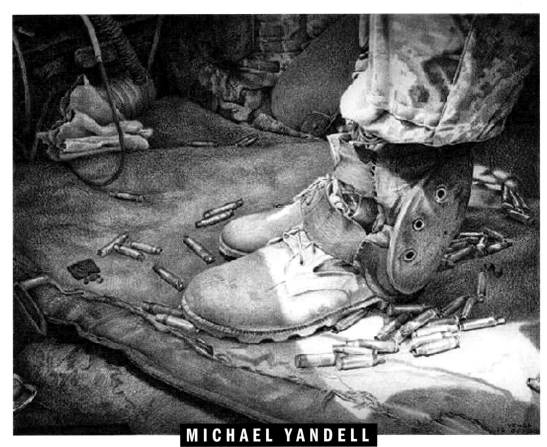

Alex Vogel,
After Action

MICHAEL YANDELL

Hope in the Void

How veterans with moral injury can help us face reality

It's April 2004 and I'm in Baghdad, anxiously waiting by our truck as my team leader takes a closer look at some ordnance our robot has deemed relatively safe. As I watch him, some kids approach me. They ask me for candy, as kids here often do. I don't have any candy,
but we have some water bottles in the truck, and they're still cool from being in the freezer at the beginning of the morning.

I think: *I'll do a good thing and give these impoverished kids some water.* So I get the water out of the truck and move to hand a

---

Michael Yandell, an Iraq War veteran and ordained minister, is pursuing a PhD at Emory University in Atlanta, Georgia.

couple of bottles to the kid in front. The boy, who's probably about eight, refuses – after all, what he asked for was candy. Something sparks inside of me. Here I am, risking life and limb, with my team leader downrange checking out an explosive, and this kid won't take something I'm offering out of the goodness of my heart.

I rip the cap off the liter bottle in my hand, dump some of it out on the ground, and throw it at him. An old man, most likely his grandfather, rushes up, grabs the boy, and pulls him away. The old man looks at me, not with anger, hate, or even sadness. His eyes are full of fear. He's afraid of *me*.

In that moment, I don't recognize that look, because I don't recognize myself. How can he be afraid of me? I'm one of the good guys, after all.

While in a prison in Nazi Germany, Dietrich Bonhoeffer wrote the poem "Who Am I?":

> Am I really what others say of me? Or am I only what I know of myself? Restless, yearning, sick, like a caged bird, struggling for life-breath, as if I were being strangled. . . . Is what remains in me like a defeated army, fleeing in disarray from victory already won?[1]

My life is nothing like Bonhoeffer's. Yet the question posed by his poem gives me pause. Who am I? I am a husband and a student. I am an ordained minister in the Christian Church (Disciples of Christ) and an aspiring theologian. I am a combat veteran, a former Explosive Ordnance Disposal specialist in the US Army. These are identities I am proud of, identities I cling to. They're how others might identify me. Yet these identities obscure another, more private identity, the something

that "remains in me like a defeated army." I am someone who bears a moral injury.

I first encountered the term "moral injury" during my studies at Brite Divinity School. According to the authors Rita Nakashima Brock and Gabriella Lettini, moral injury "comes from having transgressed one's basic moral identity and violated core moral beliefs. . . . Moral injury destroys meaning and forsakes noble causes. It sinks warriors into states of silent, solitary suffering, where bonds of intimacy and care seem impossible."[2]

Moral injury is now receiving growing attention across various disciplines as well as in clinical discourse. The concept was first introduced by clinical psychiatrist Jonathan Shay,[3] who works with veterans who have experienced trauma during and after war. According to the thorough working definition of moral injury developed in *Clinical Psychology Review*, morally injurious experiences include:

> Perpetrating, failing to prevent, bearing witness to, or learning about acts that transgress deeply held moral beliefs and expectations. . . . The individual also must be (or become) aware of the discrepancy between his or her morals and the experience (i.e., moral violation), causing dissonance and inner conflict.[4]

Moral injury has to do with questions of right and wrong. Thus it is distinct from posttraumatic stress disorder (PTSD), which is caused by experiencing life-threatening situations, not by moral conflict.

Though it's impossible to say where moral injury resides – whether in the mind, body, or

How does the church answer a soldier who says, "I am guilty"?

spirit – I believe that moral injury has much to do with the question of "who." Describing who I am requires remembering the stories that have shaped me, some of which cause me as much pain as the one above. Of course, there was more to my war experience than throwing a bottle at a young boy. There were better things, and there were worse things.

In his address to the nation on September 11, 2001, then-President George W. Bush declared, "We go forward to defend freedom and all that is good and just in our world." At the time, I thought that "we" included me, and I really believed that as part of the army I was going forward to do something good. Yet many of the memories I carried home still cause me guilt and shame.

I remember walking past bound detainees sitting in the heat indefinitely behind the building where I stayed with my team. I remember responding to calls that came in late at night to pick up weapons or ordnance, and seeing men led hooded from their homes in the dark. I remember seeing a civilian who'd been shot dead in the street one night. I do not know who shot him; he was there when we got there, and he remained there when we left. I remember when, while recovering from exposure to a chemical weapon,[5] I watched the Abu Ghraib prison scandal unfold on the news.

These memories have blurred in the time since my deployment. Nonetheless, taken together, the feeling they produce is grief. I know I am not who I thought I was. I am something different, something I never planned on being.

> Moral injury is not a veil that obscures what really happened: it is a ripping away of the veil, a permanent showing, a continuous truth-telling.

Moral injury results from exactly this kind of irreversible schism between one's perceived moral self and one's actions. A person is morally injured when she comes to recognize herself – when she has witnessed herself failing to live by her own moral convictions, especially in profoundly demanding circumstances. For veterans, this circumstance is war, however directly or indirectly it is experienced.

Simone Weil, in her essay "The Love of God and Affliction," describes affliction as something beyond and different than suffering. Rather, it's an uprooting of a life; it's something that takes hold of a person's body and soul. Weil writes: "God can never be perfectly present to us here below on account of our flesh. But [God] can be almost perfectly absent from us in extreme affliction. This is the only possibility of perfection for us on earth."[6]

Moral injury is an affliction in Weil's sense, because the schism – the moral identity crisis – at the root of moral injury is a type of moral absence. In my case, the moral self I thought I had been cultivating my whole life went missing in the moment when I saw fear in the eyes of a young boy's grandfather. In that void, God seems absent too.

Weil describes the afflicted person:

She struggles like a butterfly pinned alive into an album. But through all the horror [she] can continue to *want* to love. . . . [She] whose soul remains ever turned toward God, though the nail pierces it, finds [herself] nailed to the very center of the universe. It is the true center; it is not in the middle; it is beyond space and time;

it is God. . . . [T]his nail has pierced cleanly through all creation, through the thickness of the screen separating the soul from God.[7]

Before the war, I thought of myself as good, as someone capable of choosing goodness. I recognize now that I am not good, and that I have *never* been good in the way I once used to imagine. Yet to think that I can heal from such recognition, or that my moral injury is somehow reversible, is a false pathway to hope. Rather than returning to some glorified past, I must come to terms with who I am and then must look toward becoming something new.

Iris Murdoch writes that when we are suffering, "we console ourselves with fantasies of 'bouncing back.'"[8] Murdoch insists that, on the contrary:

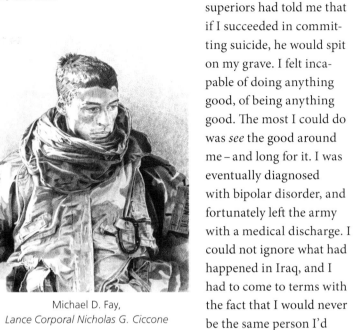

Michael D. Fay,
Lance Corporal Nicholas G. Ciccone

> We must hold on to what has really happened and not cover it with imagining how we are to unhappen it. Void makes loss a reality. . . . We have . . . a natural impulse to de-realize our world and surround ourselves with fantasy. Simply stopping this, refraining from filling voids with lies and falsity, is progress.[9]

Veterans cannot "unhappen" events. That is a fantasy in which we must not indulge. Instead, we must "hold on to what has really happened." And just what *has* really happened? What happened when I threw a bottle of water at a child? What happened when an old man saw me wearing armor, carrying a weapon, and acting angrily toward a child – and looked on me with fear? What *really* happened?

A few years after my deployment, I found myself in a psychiatric ward in Little Rock. I had cut myself. Alone in a hospital room, under the influence of a cocktail of antipsychotic drugs and sedatives, I was too tired and too ashamed to take my own life. One of my superiors had told me that if I succeeded in committing suicide, he would spit on my grave. I felt incapable of doing anything good, of being anything good. The most I could do was *see* the good around me – and long for it. I was eventually diagnosed with bipolar disorder, and fortunately left the army with a medical discharge. I could not ignore what had happened in Iraq, and I had to come to terms with the fact that I would never be the same person I'd been before the war.

I do not mean to imply that moral injury and mental illness are one and the same. After all, moral injury cannot be treated with medication, nor can it be compartmentalized. Rather, moral injury is like a nail that pierces through layers of interconnected trauma. It pierces me with a sobering clarity, illuminating not only my illness, but my entire life – past, present, and future. Thus, moral injury is not a veil that obscures what really happened: it is a ripping away of the veil, a permanent showing, a continuous truth-telling. And it hurts.

Naturally I wish that I could stop thinking, talking, and writing about moral injury. I want the fantasy to be real – I want to live my life outside of the shadow of war and of my role in it. Like other veterans, I wonder how my fellow

Americans manage so well to pretend that their lives are not deeply intertwined with ongoing global warfare. When I enrolled in an undergraduate music program after leaving the army, I used to envy other students for whom war was a distant, seemingly unconnected concept. Now, as I study theology, I wish I could pursue thoughts of God and good without seeing permanently through the lens of a past war.

I wish I could be free of the idea, which still gnaws at me, that – regardless of whatever good I may do in the future – my greatest impact on the world will be the things I did to other human beings as a young and naïve soldier. I wish I could be rid of the haunting idea that my realest self is the one I saw then. Yet having once seen into the void of moral injury, there is no unseeing it.

To find hope in the midst of moral injury, veterans must seek out encounters with people who, like us, wish to hold on to what really happened: other soldiers, teachers, mentors, family. What *really* happened when our nation indulged in a fantasy of bouncing back, of getting even, of acting with force across the globe? What really happened to those we fought? What happened to the people who sent us into combat? We must ask the hard questions and go on living, constantly turning our heads to catch a glimpse of the good – or of God.

Veterans must continue to try to articulate the void of moral injury. Their neighbors must continue to try to see it, to hear it, and to come to terms with it. There must be people and institutions capable of bearing that responsibility

> By casting all veterans as heroes, even as flawed or tragic heroes, our culture makes them easy to ignore.

in order to open pathways of hope. The church can be one of those institutions, if it makes the effort. As Bonhoeffer said in his *Ethics*:

> The church today is that community of people which is gripped by the power of the grace of Christ so that, recognizing as guilt towards Jesus Christ both its personal sin and the apostasy of the Western world from Jesus Christ, it confesses this guilt and accepts the burden of it. It is [in the church] that Jesus realizes his form in the midst of the world. That is why the church alone can be the place of personal and collective rebirth and renewal.[10]

It is clear that Bonhoeffer thought much of Jesus Christ, but this should not be taken to mean that Christianity offers the only pathway to hope. Bonhoeffer wrote of the church in this way because it was the Christian church that had so horrifically failed, in his time, to address the world around it. It was the Christian church that had failed to hold on to what really happened, that had wrapped itself in a fantasy of empire.

In our time, the Christian church and other places of faith can serve as pathways of hope through individual and collective guilt. Murdoch suggests that we can "make a spiritual use of our desolation" and that "in the more obscure labyrinths of personal relations it may be necessary to make the move which makes the void appear."[11] In places of worship, the void can be permitted to appear and can be confronted face to face.

Religious communities are unique in this ability. Will the Department of Defense or the US Army hold on to what has really happened in war? Will political leaders dispel their fantasies and meet veterans in a place of honest reflection? Certainly not. These people and institutions cannot bear the weight of it.

By casting all veterans as heroes, even as flawed or tragic heroes, our culture makes them easy to ignore. And so I offer this challenge: If a morally injured veteran walks into your house of faith and says, "I am guilty!" don't let her continue to bear her guilt alone. Don't welcome the veteran only to wrap her with fantasy, and don't try to help her unhappen what has really happened.

If a veteran enters your church, your synagogue, your mosque, or your temple, be the eyes and ears to see and hear her. Help your house of faith become deep enough, honest enough, true enough to be "the place of personal and collective rebirth and renewal" she needs. If you see that she is pinned like Weil's butterfly, alone at the center of the universe, join her there. She can show you things. ➤

1. Dietrich Bonhoeffer, *Letters and Papers from Prison, Dietrich Bonhoeffer Works, volume 8* (Minneapolis: Fortress, 2010), 459–60.

2. Rita Nakashima Brock and Gabriella Lettini, *Soul Repair: Recovering from Moral Injury after War* (Boston: Beacon Press 2012), xiv, xvi.

3. Jonathan Shay, *Achilles in Vietnam: Combat Trauma and the Undoing of Character* (New York: Scribner, 1994). Shay continues to develop the concept in *Odysseus in America: Combat Trauma and the Trials of Homecoming* (New York: Scribner, 2002).

4. Brett T. Litz, Nathan Stein, Eileen Delaney, Leslie Lebowitz, William P. Nash, Caroline Silva, Shira Maguen, "Moral Injury and Moral Repair in War Veterans: A Preliminary Model and Intervention Strategy," *Clinical Psychology Review* 29, no. 8 (December 2009): 695–706; 700.

5. C.J. Chivers, "The Secret Casualties of Iraq's Abandoned Chemical Weapons," *New York Times*, October 14, 2014.

6. Simone Weil, "The Love of God and Affliction," in *Waiting for God* (New York: Harper Perennial, 1951), 75.

7. Ibid., 81.

8. Iris Murdoch, "Void," in *Metaphysics as a Guide to Morals* (New York: Penguin Books, 1993), 502.

9. Ibid., 503.

10. Dietrich Bonhoeffer, *Ethics* (New York: Simon and Schuster, 1995), 111.

11. Murdoch, "Void," in *Metaphysics*, 503.

INSIGHT on LOVING YOUR NEIGHBOR

TERESA OF ÁVILA

It is amusing to see souls who, while they are at prayer, fancy they are willing to be despised and publicly insulted for the love of God, yet afterwards do all they can to hide their small defects. If anyone unjustly accuses them of a fault, God deliver us from their outcries! . . .

No, sisters, no; our Lord expects works from us. If you see a sick sister whom you can relieve, never fear losing your devotion; show compassion to her; if she is in pain, feel for it as if it were your own. . . . If someone else is well spoken of, be more pleased than if it were yourself; this is easy enough,

Rumiantseva Kapitolina, *Peonies*

for if you were really humble it would vex you to be praised. . . .

Beg our Lord to grant you perfect love for your neighbor, and leave the rest to him. . . . Forget your self-interests for [your neighbors'], however much nature may rebel; when opportunity occurs, take some burden upon yourself to ease your neighbor of it. Do not fancy that it will cost you nothing and that you will find it all done for you: think what the love he bore for us cost our Spouse, who, to free us from death, suffered the most painful death of all – the death of the cross. ➤

Source: *The Interior Castle*, trans. the Benedictines of Stanbrook (1921), 3.10–12.

Paula Modersohn-Becker, *Still Life with Jug*

C. S. LEWIS

In January 1942, as German bombers were terrorizing British cities, C. S. Lewis took the gospel to the airwaves, appearing repeatedly on the BBC's religious programs (the talks were later collected in the book Mere Christianity*). Increasing fame, however, did not diminish Lewis's willingess to answer the many letters he received, many as a result of his radio talks. Here he counsels a former student who is experiencing a "trough" – a time of personal difficulties.*

Caring for a Neighbor's Soul

Dear Mrs. Neylan,

Sorry you're in a trough. I'm just emerging (at least I hope I am) from a long one myself. As for the difficulty of believing it is a trough, one wants to be careful about the word "believing." We often mean by it "having confidence or assurance as a psychological state" – as we have about the existence of furniture. But that comes and goes and by no means always accompanies intellectual assent. For example, in learning to swim you believe, and even know intellectually, that water will support you, long before you feel any real confidence in the fact. . . .

In the meantime, as one has learnt to swim only by acting on the assent in the teeth of all instinctive conviction, so we shall proceed to faith only by acting as if we had it. Adapting a passage in *The Imitation of Christ* [Thomas à Kempis], one can say: "What would I do now if I had a full assurance that there was only a temporary trough," and having got the answer, go and do it.

I am a man, and therefore lazy: you a woman, therefore probably a fidget. So it may be good to advise you (though it would be bad to me) not even to try to do in the trough all you can do on the peak. . . .

I know all about the despair of overcoming chronic temptations. It is not serious, provided self-offended petulance, annoyance at breaking records, impatience, etc. doesn't get the upper hand. No amount of falls will really undo us if we keep on picking ourselves up each time.

We shall of course be very muddy and tattered children by the time we reach home. But the bathrooms are all ready, the towels put out, and the clean linen clothes are in the airing cupboard. The only fatal thing is to lose one's temper and give up. It is when we notice the dirt that God is most present to us: it is the very sign of his presence. ➤

JOHN STOTT

"As the Father has sent me, even so I send you." —John 20:21

We have two instructions of Jesus – a great commandment, "love your neighbor," and a great commission, "go and make disciples." What is the relation between the two? Some of us behave as if we thought them identical, so that if we share the gospel with somebody, we consider we have completed our responsibility to love him or her. But no. The Great Commission neither explains, nor exhausts, nor supersedes the Great Commandment. What it does is to add to the requirement of neighbor-love and neighbor-service a new and urgent Christian dimension. If we truly love our neighbor, we shall without a doubt share with him or her the good news of Jesus. How can we possibly claim to love our neighbor if we know the gospel but keep it from them?

Equally, however, if we truly love our neighbor we shall not stop with evangelism. Our neighbor is neither a bodiless soul that we should love only their soul, nor a soulless body that we should care for its welfare alone, nor even a body-soul isolated from society. God created the human person, who is my neighbor, as a body-soul-in-community. Therefore, if we love our neighbors as God made them, we must inevitably be concerned for their total welfare, the good of their soul, their body, and their community.

Moreover, it is this vision of the human person as a social being that obliges us to add a *political* dimension to our social concern. Humanitarian activity cares for the casualties of a sick society. We should be concerned with preventive medicine or community health as well, which means the quest for better social structures in which peace, dignity, freedom, and justice are secured for all. And there is no reason why, in pursuing this quest, we should not join hands with all people of good will, even if they are not Christians.

To sum up, we are sent into the world, like Jesus, to serve: "I am among you as one who serves" (Luke 22:27). For this is the natural expression of our love for our neighbors. We love. We go. We serve. And in this we have (or should have) no ulterior motive. . . . Love has no need to justify itself. It merely expresses itself in service wherever it sees need. . . .

Social action, then, is *a partner of evangelism.* As partners the two belong to each other and yet are independent of each other. Each stands on its own feet in its own right alongside the other. Neither is a means to the other, or even a manifestation of the other, for each is an end in itself. Both are expressions of unfeigned love. Evangelism and compassionate service belong together in the mission of God. ➤

Evangelism versus Neighbor-Love?

Taken from John Stott's classic *Christian Mission in the Modern World,* which has been newly expanded and revised by Christopher J. H. Wright (IVP Books, 2015). Wright is the international ministries director at the Langham Partnership, the London-based mission fellowship that Stott founded in 1969. *www.langham.org*

MATTHEW LOFTUS

A boy plays in the Sandtown neighborhood of Baltimore, where Freddie Gray was arrested.

Needing My Neighbor

A young physician moves to West Baltimore eager to help a broken community – and finds himself relying on his new neighbors to help conquer his own addiction.

"I've always wanted to help people." My medical school application essay opened with those words, and when I came to Baltimore at age twenty to start my medical training, I was dead-set on helping people in Africa. After two years of attending church in the Sandtown-Winchester neighborhood, though, I fell in love with the community, so my wife and I decided to move into the neighborhood in 2009. I admired the work my church there was doing to deal with the poverty, racism, and institutional neglect

Sandtown was known for. (It became even more well-known for these ills in April 2015 when Freddie Gray suffered his fatal injury here.)

I helped to start a community mental health program with the church while also participating in other ministries. After finishing my residency, I found a great job at a community health center that allowed me to balance vocation, family, and advocacy. Our fellow church members, poor as they were, joined forces to bless the even less fortunate by sending us overseas to a maternity and pediatric hospital in South Sudan.

In my work in Sandtown, it felt good to be helping others as I had always wanted to do, loving my neighbor in word and deed. Yet I felt unable to help myself.

I remember the day my hands started to shake as I walked the two blocks from my main office to our satellite location. This other office, I knew, had unfiltered, unprotected wireless internet, and simply thinking about the ease with which I could access pornography there made me feel nauseated. I reached in my pocket for my phone to call a friend and community leader, Elder, as he is known in Sandtown.

"I just need you to pray for me. I'm feeling really tempted," I said.

"I will pray for you, brother, but I want you to think about our community," he said, as he nearly always did when I called.

Like many other young do-gooders, I began my ministry work full of idealism and quickly met the harsh realities of inner-city life. The church that Elder started several decades ago works closely with mine, guided by the same principles of Christian community development pioneered by the civil rights hero John Perkins, and we often shared our frustrations

about addressing the issues that have made Sandtown infamous. Helping people here isn't easy, and for a long time, "thinking about the community" meant thinking about my failures and shortcomings. Sure, I'd had some successes over the years, but I'd also learned how persistent the stigma and shame of mental health issues could be in a community like ours, and how devious Satan could be in destroying the lives of the people I was investing in.

The struggle I was experiencing the day I called Elder mirrored what I'd seen my neighbors go through in dealing with their own mental illness and addictions. I found myself making the same excuses about getting help I'd heard them make, yet I was still faster to recognize their pride than my own. All the same, I worried that neither they nor I could ever get better, and I felt ashamed that my desire to love my neighbor did not extend to the people on my computer screen, or to my wife, to whom I had vowed to be faithful. While I had struggled with pornography since I was a teenager, in the course of my time in Sandtown, I'd begun using it more and more – a response to my anxiety about how much good I was really doing in my efforts to help the neighborhood. In effect, I was asking pornography to cover up my inability to be the perfect Christian social justice advocate. Though I knew I had a problem, to myself I justified my half-heartedness in the battle for purity by holding up the good works I was doing (or trying to do). My addiction held such power over me that I had grown accustomed to hiding the depth of my brokenness even from myself.

Like most people, I far preferred to offer help than receive it. But my decision to reach out to

---

Matthew Loftus lives with his wife and two children in South Sudan, where he teaches and practices family medicine. Visit matthewandmaggie.org *to learn more about his work.*

Elder turned out to be a game-changer. After I confessed my sin in our Bible study, he invited me to meet more regularly with other people from the neighborhood to help conquer my addiction. As I submitted to his spiritual direction and let myself be accountable to him, he helped me to see a different way of relating to the neighborhood. He shared many of his own struggles and feelings of inadequacy, and by doing this, he modeled how I could think about my community and pray for my neighbors in a way that expected God to work regardless of my efforts. When I reoriented my heart toward loving Christ first, it was much easier to see that my self-perceived failures could not stop his work in redeeming his people.

Most decent addiction programs recognize the need for a holistic approach, in part because it's so clear how the barbed hooks of addiction embed themselves in a person's mind, body, spirit, and community. The importance of good friends, stable work or hobbies, regular exercise, a good diet, and spiritual discipline is routinely emphasized by practitioners and therapists who understand how a patient's day-to-day life differs from the few hours a week they spend together. Still, despite the many psychiatrists and pastors who appreciate this reality, I often hear from patients how a trusted authority breezily denied or ignored either the biochemical or the spiritual dimension of their illness. What's more, despite noble exceptions, not enough recovery programs recognize how poverty puts the recommended practices of self-care out of many addicts' reach.

The first step for those of us seeking to serve broken neighborhoods, then, is to avoid the temptation to self-importantly distance ourselves from those we are helping. Wealth and privilege can blind us to the spiritual realities that shape all disease (not just mental illness).

The Enlightenment worldview that comes with a professional degree pushes us to treat addiction and mental illness as wholly biochemical processes that are suffered passively. The treatment, we too easily believe, lies in submitting to pharmaceutical modification and professional therapy. While well-intentioned, we may fail to realize that our attitude is just as simplistic as our less "enlightened" neighbors' belief that mental illness and addiction are purely a matter of sinfulness or spiritual oppression, unconnected with the body.

In fact, both approaches – the modern scientific impulse to define every injurious behavior as "addictive," as well as the reactionary tendency to deny that there's anything biochemically mediated about plain old sinfulness – fall short in describing most people's experience of addiction. Sin begins in our hearts, minds, and souls, to be sure, but it almost always spreads to our tongues, hands, and genitals, so that even our brains are physically reshaped (most obviously in the case of drug addiction). As a result, addicts usually suffer from a combination of basic human sinfulness, paralyzing social shame, and the ugly feedback of brain chemistry, with no bright lines marking where one category ends and another begins.

Accordingly, when people seek healing, we should recognize how important it is to bring all aspects of a person's life to light so that we may bring every possible resource to bear: community support, regular accountability, prayer, pharmaceutical treatment (if indicated), and careful discussion with a professional. Most people – including myself – need to acknowledge both the physical and spiritual dimensions of their addiction in order to begin to fully recover. Furthermore, while loneliness, poverty, and abuse do predispose people to addiction and other mental illnesses, it is

foolhardy to suppose that addressing these issues will somehow magically cure a person's addiction. Overzealous writers, politicians, and policy makers often proclaim that the answer is simple: addiction will be solved by medication, or better community programs, or prayer, or more jobs. There are too many addicts who are medicated, friendly, and spiritual for any of these theories to be true.

In our urban mental health ministry, one place we've seen real successes is a support group that uses participatory learning methods adopted from the Community Health Evangelism program. Through this group, church members work together to find a holistic understanding of their minds and bodies, one that draws from the Bible while incorporating insights from medical science and psychology. Given that many people are hesitant to seek formal counseling and don't want to roll the dice with whatever pharmaceutical cocktail a psychiatrist might prescribe, groups like this hold great potential for meeting the needs of hurting people in vulnerable communities. In addition, they enable participants who would benefit from medications or counseling to get to know others who can help them gain access to what they need.

The second step for those of us seeking to serve impoverished communities is just as crucial: we must acknowledge our patients' strengths and recognize how they can serve us. By offering them the power to ask hard questions and to hold us accountable, we can learn to grow together with them spiritually. This helps us look up to those who can help us, not just down to those we can assist.

Though I began my career intent on helping others, it wasn't until I learned to submit to my neighbors and to accept their help that I recognized how I'd been holding out for the sake of my pride, allowing my desire to be a helper

to overtake my love for Christ. Of course, one does not have to be struggling with sexual sin, addiction, or mental illness to benefit from this sort of honesty and accountability. Still, demonstrating vulnerability and asking for accountability in just these areas is especially powerful in building trust and strengthening relationships. After all, so many of our neighbors in broken communities are struggling with these problems too.

The longer I prayed with my new friends from the neighborhood, the deeper our sense of solidarity became. There are countless ways in which my race, class, and background give me privileges that they don't have, but at the foot of the cross the only privilege that mattered was being one with Christ. I couldn't pull rank; the questions Elder asked me in our weekly counseling sessions – questions that in many cases he'd learned from Gordon Cosby (1917–2013), founder of the Church of the Saviour in Washington, DC – disarmed my excuses and forced me to find ways to keep my promises.

Regardless of our level of wealth or privilege, those of us who want to serve the poor must learn to allow the line between helper and helped to dissolve. As human beings, our minds, bodies, and spirits inextricably work together – or are broken together. For all of us, the beginning of healing is to face our problems with the help of others, in community. By learning to see our neighbors not as objects of pity but as fellow image-bearers – brothers and sisters whom we can serve and be served by – we become better able to guide one another to Christ. ⤸

> The beginning of healing is to face our problems with the help of others, in community.

The Coming of the King

Laura E. Richards

Illustrated by Jennifer Gneiting

S OME CHILDREN WERE AT PLAY in their playground one day when a herald rode through the town, blowing a trumpet and crying aloud, "The king! The king passes by on this road today. Make ready for the king!"

This short story is taken from Easter Stories: Classic Tales for the Holy Season *(Plough, 2015).* *"This thoughtfully curated collection is remarkable for its range and breadth . . . A reminder of the great Easter themes of transformation, reconciliation, and the triumph of life over death"* (National Catholic Register). www.plough.com

The children stopped their play and looked at one another. "Did you hear that?" they said. "The king is coming. He may look over the wall and see our playground; who knows? We must put it in order."

The playground was sadly dirty, and in the corners were scraps of paper and broken toys, for these were careless children. But now, one brought a hoe, and another a rake, and a third ran to fetch the wheelbarrow from behind the garden gate. They labored hard till at length all was clean and tidy.

"Now it is clean!" they said. "But we must make it pretty, too, for kings are used to fine things; maybe he would not notice mere cleanness, for he may have it all the time."

Then one brought sweet rushes and strewed them on the ground, others made garlands of oak leaves and pine tassels and hung them on the walls, and the littlest one pulled marigold buds and threw them all about the playground, "to look like gold," he said.

When all was done, the playground was so beautiful that the children stood and looked at it and clapped their hands with pleasure.

"Let us keep it always like this!" said the littlest one; and the others cried, "Yes! Yes! That is what we will do."

They waited all day for the coming of the king, but he never came; only towards sunset a man with travel-worn clothes and a kind, tired face passed along the road and stopped to look over the wall.

"What a pleasant place!" said the man. "May I come in and rest, dear children?"

The children brought him in gladly and set him on the seat that they had made out of an old cask. They had covered it with an old red cloak to make it look like a throne, and it made a very good one.

"It is our playground," they said. "We made it pretty for the king, but he did not come, and now we mean to keep it so for ourselves."

"That is good," said the man.

"Because we think pretty and clean is nicer than ugly and dirty!" said another.

"That is better," said the man.

"And for tired people to rest in," said the littlest one.

"That is best of all!" said the man.

He sat and rested, and looked at the children with such kind eyes that they came about him and told him all they knew – about the five puppies in the barn, and the thrush's nest with four blue eggs, and the shore where the gold shells grew; and the man nodded and understood all about it.

By and by he asked for a cup of water, and they brought it to him in the best cup, the one with the gold sprigs on it. Then he thanked the children and rose and went on his way; but before he went he laid his hand on their heads for a moment, and the touch went warm to their hearts.

The children stood by the wall and watched the man as he went slowly along. The sun was setting, and the light fell in long slanting rays across the road.

"He looks so tired," said one of the children.

"But he was so kind," said another.

"See!" said the littlest one. "How the sun shines on his hair! It looks like a crown of gold." ➤

Bruno Liljefors, *Common Swifts*

No One Wrings the Air Dry

1

Seeping, like swollen eyelids
behind Burney Falls,
a dozen nests daub the cliff.
Mother Swift is a black knife
thrust sidewise, the maul of water
rent. Shred-by-strand,
her cargo of moss jeweled
by the mist, she stalls
mid-air: Stone Sweet Home,
slicked over with spit.

2

In the streaming darkness
the slow, exacting language of eggs.

3

No lulling pulse, or voice –
chicks in their shells wake
to endless tumult. Pure roar.
Where warmth hovers,
each day's solace is juiced
with spiders and gnats,
bees, beetles. Whatever it takes.

4

Hour by hour, the breached
torrent. The killing cold.
For each shivering life,
she is the preening beak.

5

First hop's a doozy. Readied
for iridescence, her offspring
brave the shock of quiet,
dry air, and daylight. They carry,
from this flight forward, night's
living sheen in their hollow bones.

LAURIE KLEIN

Marc Chagall, *The Sacrifice of Isaac*, Musée National Marc Chagall, Nice, France

Does Faith Breed Violence?

Rabbi Jonathan Sacks probes the shared roots
of Judaism, Christianity, and Islam.

NATHANIEL PETERS

Old secularization theories die hard. The twenty-first century was supposed to be a new age of enlightenment in which progressive politics and bourgeois economics domesticated religion, family, and bonds of national kinship, making us morally unencumbered global citizens. Then came ISIS, Boko Haram, and

The Sacrifice of Ishmael, eighteenth-century fresco
in the Haft Tanan Museum, Shiraz, Iran

theological problem ("What ISIS Really Wants," March 2015). Whatever the influence of economics or other factors, their followers are driven by a particular theology with a particular – albeit minority – pedigree and roots in Islam. Wood is right: Islamic extremism is a theological problem. But how do we go about solving it? The solution to the theological problem must be theological, not military. And the best proposal to date comes from Rabbi Lord Jonathan Sacks, former chief rabbi of the United Kingdom.

Not in God's Name is primarily a work of ancient biblical interpretation, but

other representatives of the vicious new wave of Islamic extremism. More surprising than the brutality and violence of their crimes is the way these groups have infiltrated our society. Why do young people who should be enjoying the fruits of liberal democracy become radicalized? Much of our intellectual elite does not see religion as a significant factor in human society and history. For them, the answer to this question must be economic or social – hence President Obama's persistent assertion that, despite its own claims to the contrary, ISIS is not an Islamic or theological problem.

But as the violence mounts and as men and women who are neither poor nor culturally marginalized commit mass atrocities, the heads have begun to come out of the sand. In one of the most read and debated articles of the past year, Graeme Wood argued in *The Atlantic* that ISIS and Boko Haram are a

it begins with contemporary social theory. Sacks calls evil committed in the name of a sacred cause "altruistic evil," the kind that turns "ordinary non-psychopathic people into cold-blooded murderers." They slaughter with delight, confident that they are doing God's work. The problem is not religion, per se; as the twentieth century's body count from totalitarian regimes makes clear, substitutes for religion lead to more violence. Rather, it comes from two factors: our "groupishness" – the fact that we are dependent, relational animals – and dualism. Our social nature leads us not only to altruism (usually directed toward members of our group), but also to suspicion and aggression toward outsiders.

Religion is implicated as the most powerful source of group identity many have. And religion offers a way to explain why the world is not as it should be. If these explanations retain

Nathaniel Peters is a doctoral candidate in historical theology at Boston College.

a complexity matching the world's, they can be healthy. The problem arises, Sacks argues, when they become pathologically dualistic – when the evil in the world is monochromatically attributed to "them." This kind of dualism dehumanizes opponents and allows believers to see themselves always as victims, irrespective of evidence to the contrary.

What is it that makes dualism pathological? Here Sacks borrows from the French theorist René Girard (1923–2015), who argued that societies begin with murder and violence between two figures or groups. The most effective way to resolve that violence, according to Girard, is to blame it on a third, the scapegoat. Sacrificing the outsider allows both sides to feel that justice has been done, but not at the expense of either group. Religion performs the important task of casting out and ending the violence that would otherwise rend society asunder. But Girard's theory has a second part. The violence comes in the first place from mimetic desire: desire that imitates the desire of another (think of Cain and Abel). Sibling rivalry – the desire to have what your brother has and be what he is – lies at the heart of our conflicts.

Sacks sees this sibling rivalry at the heart of the relations between Judaism, Christianity, and Islam. Believers of each faith feel that within humanity God has a favored son or chosen people, and they fight other claimants who would rob them of God's paternal love. Paul claims that faith in Jesus, not Jewish ancestry, makes one a child of God's promise. Islam incorporates both Judaism and Christianity into its understanding of salvation. Meanwhile the Hebrew Scriptures' view of sibling rivalry seems straightforward: Ishmael is sent away, and Isaac is blessed; Jacob have I

Not in God's Name: Confronting Religious Violence, Jonathan Sacks (Schocken Books)

loved, but Esau have I hated. Below the surface, however, a deeper and different interpretation lies hidden. In order to overcome this sibling rivalry, Sacks argues, we need to look at these texts anew and read them as we have not read them before. Or, to be more precise, we need to read them as the great rabbis and Talmudists did. Accordingly, in the book's remaining pages, Sacks offers rabbinic commentary on Genesis and suggests ways of applying it to conflicts in our own time.

Before getting into further detail, it is necessary to step back and see what Sacks has done. First, he has accepted contemporary accounts of how human evolution gave rise to our ethical and philosophical frameworks. But, unlike many scientists and philosophers, Sacks does not see religion, traditional morality, and the particular bonds of family and nation as evolutionary stages to outgrow. Instead, he sees them as the solution to our fundamental problems. He knows that we need meaning, identity, and purpose – the very things that secularism would undo. Likewise, Sacks shows that the solution to bad theology is not to secularize it. He does not call for an acid bath of historical criticism for the Quran or for an unmasking of the power dynamics behind the Bible, but rather for reading scripture within an ongoing tradition. We do not need more demythologizing; we need true myths.

Sacks then walks through the stories of Abraham, Isaac, Jacob, and Joseph to show that God does choose some for his covenant, but never rejects those not chosen. Many biblical scholars see these stories as the justification for Israel's conquest of the land of their neighbors.

Esau is the father of the Edomites, future enemies of Israel, and God's rejection of Esau serves as justification for fighting the Edomites. Sacks takes a different tack. Instead of vilifying Ishmael and Esau, he argues, the text makes us feel a deep sympathy for them – and we are told that God responds in the same way. Isaac may receive the covenant, but Ishmael remains Abraham's son and will be blessed accordingly. Much of the story of Abraham's descendants focuses on the unlikely election of the least and weakest. Instead of choosing the strong older son – Esau, for example – the obvious choice in the eyes of the world, God chooses the younger mama's boy. The message is two-fold. First, "Israel is the people whose achievements are transparently God-given. What for others is natural, for Israel is the result of divine intervention. Israel must be weak if it is to be strong, for its strength must come from heaven." Second, Isaac's election does not mean Ishmael's rejection. God has particular blessings for Ishmael and Esau. In the stories of election, "God rejects rejection."

Sacks goes on to treat the story of the Exodus, in which Israel learns to care for the stranger and the vulnerable by itself becoming vulnerable. He briefly examines the so-called hard texts of the Old Testament, arguing that war becomes an option for Israel only when the opportunities for peace have been exhausted. Moreover, unlike the cultures of classical antiquity, Israel never seeks honor and glory on the battlefield. Consistent monotheism responds to evil not with blame, but with penitence: "The first focuses on external cause, the second on internal response. Blame looks to the past, penitence to the future. Blame is passive, penitence active. A penitential culture is constructed on the logic of responsibility. If bad things happen to us, it is up to us to put them right."

Christians reading Sacks will be greatly edified, particularly when they discover unfamiliar modes of rabbinic exegesis. Moreover, they will find an advocate. Sacks is one of the few public figures to call the destruction of Christian communities in the Middle East "the religious equivalent of ethnic cleansing," and "one of the crimes against humanity of our time." He writes of the history of anti-Semitism with care and nuance. He barely mentions Jesus – or Girard's argument that the crucifixion unmasks the scapegoat mechanism – but finds Saint Paul very troubling. In a sense, Sacks's book is a sustained response to Paul's argument that faith in Jesus, not Jewish birth, is what makes one part of the chosen people. Sacks wants to show that Paul's anxiety is misplaced, suggesting that even if God does not choose Gentiles in the same way as Israel, neither does he reject them. Implicitly, Sacks wants Christianity and Islam to become more Jewish: more aware of their own cultural particularity and less aimed at evangelistic claims of universal religious truth. This is perhaps the deepest point of incomprehension between Jews and Christians. Christians can join Sacks in saying no to religious hatred, but they cannot back away from the implications of the cross and resurrection.

That said, Christians should be grateful to Sacks for what he says and how he says it. Sacks connects the great traditions of scriptural interpretation to contemporary social theory. He offers theological solutions to theological problems. He makes a significant contribution to the conversation that needs to take place between traditional Jews, Christians, and Muslims. This is vital, for it is from these communities that the solution to religious violence will come. ⇸

Strangers Drowning
Larissa MacFarquhar
(Penguin Press)

Who would refuse to help a drowning stranger? Yet in a globalized world where starving children are always within reach (at least of our donations), that's essentially what most of us do, reasoning that we can't save everyone. MacFarquhar gravitates to the exceptions: the people who spare nothing to help others. After Hector and Sue Badeau adopt two children, social services ask them to take another; they end up with twenty-two. Baba Amte finds a leper dying at the roadside, and winds up founding a community for hundreds. For some of those profiled, doing good becomes compulsive; others burn out. MacFarquhar tells their stories sympathetically, probing why our society has given do-gooders such a bad rap. True, the danger of hubris is real: untethered from faith in God, attempts at world-saving ultimately lead to despair. Yet – as we learn from Francis of Assisi, Damien of Molokai, or Teresa of Calcutta – extremism in compassion is no vice. And so: what about us?

Portraits: John Berger on Artists
John Berger,
edited by Tom Overton
(Verso)

"I have always hated being called an art critic," writes John Berger, whose *Ways of Seeing* (1972) helped redefine art criticism. To Berger, art is never divorced from life, especially the life of those living at the margins. Here, in chronological order, he profiles seventy-four artists, from the Chauvet cave painters to a Palestinian artist born in 1983. His political commitments are reflected even in the book's format: the illustrations are black-and-white, "because glossy color reproductions in the consumerist world of today tend to reduce what they show to items in a luxury brochure for millionaires." The vivid, down-to-earth profiles, written in the form of essays, interviews, travelogues, and letters, make lavish illustrations beside the point. Berger is a storyteller who cuts through fine art's privileged trappings to the human reality beneath. A Marxist, he is certainly no religious believer, and his views are a mixed bag. Even so, his observations, for instance on Piero della Francesco's *Resurrection,* are often revelatory. At his best, he helps us to *see,* truly and with love, our fellow human beings.

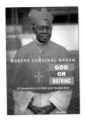

God or Nothing:
A Conversation on Faith
with Nicolas Diat
Robert Cardinal Sarah
(Ignatius)

Born to an animist family in a mud hut in West Africa, Robert Sarah hardly seemed a likely future leader in the Catholic Church. In this wide-ranging interview with a French journalist, he tells his surprising story, reflecting on the seven popes he has served under and offering thoughts on evangelism, prayer, marriage and sexuality, and the future of the church. He defends Catholic teaching with blunt forthrightness – "a woman cardinal is as ridiculous as the idea of a priest who wanted to become a nun" – but he combines this with self-criticism: "Both the clergy and the laity today are in urgent need of conversion." Nor can the cardinal be pigeon-holed as liberal or conservative in his witness to the gospel: "There is never any more authentic relation with God than in an encounter with the poor. For this is the source of life in God: poverty. Our Father is poor. This is perhaps an image of God that eludes us and repels us, because we have not really met 'the Son of man [who] has nowhere to lay his head' (Matt. 8:20)." While the book addresses many issues particular to Catholics, here is rich spiritual fare for all Christians. ➤ *The Editors*

Vasilij Ivanovic Surikov, *Young Woman at Prayer*

The Danger of Prayer

By all means, pray. But be careful what you ask for.

EBERHARD ARNOLD

When we call on God, we are asking him to do something that we cannot, to bring into being something that we ourselves do not know how to create. We are seeking for the impossible to happen, for something to be changed irrevocably that we could never change. We are asking for a history to unfold for which we ourselves could never be responsible.

The question is: Do we have the faith that through our prayer the status quo can be shattered? Can we believe that at our call Christ will come among us to judge and save? When we ask for the Holy Spirit, are we ready for God to strike us like a burst of flaming lightning, so that at last we experience Pentecost? Do we really believe that God's kingdom is imminent?

Are we capable of believing that through our pleading this kingdom will break in? Are we able to believe that as a result of our prayer the entire history of the world will be turned topsy-turvy?

Let us come to God in the absolute certainty that Jesus' words are true: "The kingdom of God has drawn near!" and, "If you have faith, nothing will be impossible for you." Wonders will occur, mountains will be torn from their place, and the whole situation as it is on earth will be changed. Mighty things will happen when we have faith.

It is dangerous to call on God in this way, for it means we are ready, not only to be lifted up from our place, but to be hurled down from our place. So let us concentrate all our powers on Jesus' nearness, on the silent coming of the Holy Spirit, ready for everything to be changed by his intervention.

Prayer must never supplant work. If we sincerely ask God for his will to be done, for his nature to be revealed in our work, for his rule to bring humankind to unity, justice, and love, then our life will be one of work. Faith without works is dead. Prayer without work is hypocrisy. Unless we actively work to build up God's kingdom, the Lord's Prayer – "Your kingdom come" – is a lie on our lips. The purpose of Jesus' prayer is to bring us to the point where its meaning is lived out, where it actually happens and becomes part of history. Each of us needs to find a way to devote our whole working strength so that God is honored, his will is done, and his kingdom comes. Unless our love for Jesus results in deeds, our connection to the Tree of Life will wither.

In addition, if we are going to endure the weight of evil and suffering in this world, we must not only ask God to forgive our sins, but that he would grant us the love that forgives everyone all the evil they have done to us. . . .

If our prayer is genuine, if we really want nothing but the kingdom of God, then we will think of all the regions of the world. We will call on God to intervene in the history of the nations, the history of classes and ranks, the history that has brought injustice to a climax. We will call on him to come with his judgment and to let his righteousness and peace break in like the dawn. This should be our prayer and the prayer of the church. ⤳

Taken from Eberhard Arnold's The Prayer God Answers, *newly released by Plough with an introduction by Richard J. Foster,* www.plough.com

Eberhard Arnold
An Appreciation

RICHARD J. FOSTER

From the introduction to Arnold's book The Prayer God Answers *(Plough, 2016):*

Eberhard Arnold's astonishing ministry occurred in Germany between the enormous upheavals of World War I and World War II. His major work, *Innerland*, absorbed his energies for most of his life. The manuscript had to be packed in metal boxes and buried at night for safekeeping from the Nazis, who raided his study on two occasions. *Innerland* spoke forcefully against the demonic spirits that animated German society in that day: the murderous strains of racism and bigotry, the heady nationalistic fervor, the mindless mass hysteria, and the vulgar materialism.

In 1933 the Bruderhof, the intentional Christian community that Arnold had founded, was stormed by the Gestapo, SS, and police; and its school was closed. Ultimately the Bruderhof community was forced to flee Nazi oppression, first to Liechtenstein and then to England. Today Bruderhof communities can be found in several countries around the world.

In the midst of this tumultuous era in human history, Arnold penned his lucid and wise essay, *The Prayer God Answers.* In it he traverses the landscape of Christian prayer, providing us with vital and hard-won insights into the life of faith. ⤳

Richard J. Foster is the founder of Renovaré, an ecumical Christian community, and the author of several books including A Celebration of Discipline *(Harper San Francisco, 1988).*

Gripped by the Infinite

A Young Woman's Journey to Faith

ANNEMARIE WÄCHTER

orn in a village in eastern Germany in 1909, Annemarie Wächter encountered ideas and people in her adolescence that unsettled her and disturbed the simple faith of her childhood. Like countless young people before and since, she spent her young adulthood trying to make sense of the world. Collected in the book Anni *(ed. Marianne Wright and Erna Albertz, Plough), her letters and diary entries describe, with startling honesty and deep sensitivity, how a young woman who had been allergic to claims of absolute truth found her way to faith and a meaningful vocation within a Christian community.*

Anni's roommate at college was Emi-Margret Arnold, who described to Anni the Bruderhof, a community that her parents, Eberhard and Emmy Arnold, had established near Fulda, Germany. Anni later recounted:

mi-Margret told me some of the inner back-ground of the community she came from, but I could not understand it. I sensed that she had a real belief in God, a firm basis, and that is what we mostly discussed, but I was afraid of it. I wanted to be very sure that this really was the truth and that I would not find out, after a year or two, that it had given the appearance of being real when it actually was not. So I was somewhat critical, even though in another way I was attracted. I did not want to bind myself to any firm belief or to commit myself.

As she entered her twenties, Anni's discontent and seeking intensified.

Diary, November 10, 1929
I would just like to know whether it's really different for us than for mature people – I mean those people who really stand for something and who don't simply exist. It must be strange to have a worldview. What does believing and not believing mean anyway? What is religion, and who has it? Where do great people get their beliefs from, their conviction? Have they had an experience of God? Tillich says, "Youth means being gripped by the infinite, and therefore youth is religion." Who is it that is gripped? We can't believe anything anymore, because we know too much. Everything has its name and is classified and arranged neatly in its place. Of course, people say that to be eternally seeking and not finding means an incomplete development, but to me it still seems the best option. Who can dare commit herself to a certain course for the whole length of life?

Diary, June 28, 1930
This is true objectivity: to be able to conquer your own self enough that you can acknowledge what is right, and then to fight for that with your whole inner arsenal. No one grows through neutrality; the only result is insipidity and nonsensical philosophizing. It just makes you stupid. This type of inner loneliness is the worst thing there is. Sometimes it could kill you.

Diary, April 3, 1931
It has been almost a year since I wrote in here. And what has happened since then? Much and nothing. It seems as if the world has come to a standstill for me because of the weakening relationships with those my own age and with other people in general.

In spring of 1931, Emi-Margret invited Anni to visit her at the community. Anni processed the experience in a letter to her friend.

April 14, 1931
Dear Emi-Margret,

It is horribly hard to put things into words, and especially deeply held thoughts. I have a great horror of all emotional outpourings and public displays of the depths of the soul. So to be able to say something like this that is personal and yet objective is not so simple. You may have wondered why I was completely quiet while I was with you all. But you can't say a lot when something overwhelms you completely. Since the time in my teens when I had a sense of fulfillment from true fellowship between people, I had never again experienced anything like that. That is now quite a number of years ago. There was always a lot of talking and reading and chattering about it, especially at school, but no one believed in it. . . . And in spite of all you told me about your community, I really didn't believe in it either.

You say so simply, "We believe in the message Christ brings of the community of all people in one spirit," and then you act accordingly. And it is actual and living – there is no discussion or babbling, no senseless philosophizing. This made me very happy. Do you understand what I mean? If you don't believe in anything, it would be terrible to commit yourself to something. Life still wouldn't have any real significance.

You probably thought it was strange that I don't have any plans for the near future and that I am stepping out into the world in such an indifferent way. What's the use of further

Anni in the simple garb of the German Youth Movement

studies? I have a holy terror of anything abstract, as much as I also unfortunately have a weakness for it, as you well know. Well, up to now my whole theory has been a complete washout. And what besides? I truly don't know. But please don't think that I am about to raise my voice in lamentation and pity myself a little. It is only a somewhat unpleasant fact.   *Anni*

Several months later, Anni visited the Bruderhof again. As she later described:

I had no understanding of the Christian basis of the community. I was a Protestant by birth, but inwardly the Christian faith had no meaning for me. On the contrary, because I felt that there was so much hypocrisy, I had turned against it. But during my visit, there was a meeting that impressed me. I do not know what the meeting was about, but I can only say that something of the Holy Spirit was moving there. It gripped me, and I felt: I have to come back here! I have to stay here!

Diary, June 26, 1931
When will I go to Emi-Margret's community to stay? Nothing else seems important to me anymore. But I know that it will then be a matter of either-or. Since spring, I haven't moved one step forward. Can I go this way? I believe that I have in some way felt the Spirit, and yet I haven't found the courage to come

to a decision. I feel embarrassed when people speak about the coming of and hope for God's kingdom. I am ashamed of reading the Bible. I don't understand any of it – I mean, I am not able to believe in it.

Anni arrived for an extended visit to the community in early January 1932. A month later, she wrote to her family.

February 6, 1932
My dear Mama, Hilde, and Reinhold,

It is a community of people from the most varied classes and professions, who have come out of groups with the most diverse world outlooks. They wish to live and work – and are even ready to die – for one common goal. The one and only thing to which they feel themselves bound is contained in the words of the Bible, especially the New Testament. They feel deeply gripped by and committed to what comes to us through the Bible from God, the coming of his kingdom, the sending out of his Holy Spirit, the life of Jesus, and what he requires of humankind. This compelled them to such a degree that they had to break off their former lives in order to place their entire lives and whole strength from then on into the service of discipleship to Christ.

This will be especially difficult to understand in our time in which there are so few people willing to live and die in a manner consistent with their convictions. The community members believe in God and his Trinity as an absolute reality. He is the first and the last Truth. He is reality; there is none greater. To them, he is neither a beautiful ideal arising from the affectations of the emotional life nor an indeterminate, problematic entity. God is love, faithfulness, grace, mercy, and justice. God loves all people as his children, and no one is greater than another. That is why all people should love each other as brothers and sisters.

It is not possible to create a life of love and brotherliness within the fragmentation of the existing social order. The communal way of life alone can foster such relationships. It is not always easy to recognize the brother in every man, and not believe oneself higher and better than another. Living by love implies a life of social justice, because love encompasses each person equally – it cannot show partiality. And economic injustice can be accepted just as little as human injustice. Such a community must reject capitalism and desire to live in complete community of goods, in the communism of the original apostolic church. Personal property and earnings are completely renounced.

And because all here are conscious of the difficulty and bitterness of the way, there is no sweetly gushing Christianity, no false enthusiasm that fades into thin air with empty phrases (as one may be tempted to think), but rather a Christianity of true conviction and faith, and therefore a Christianity of deeds. That is the pivotal thing. As part of its ultimate goal and through the strength of God and his spirit, this Christianity seeks to penetrate the whole of life right down into the smallest practical details. It is precisely in the most mundane routines of daily life – those that are not filled by the elation of holier hours – that this Christianity must be tested, lest it remain empty and useless.

I only hope that through this letter you are able to understand a little of how I came to this decision, and that it is impossible for me to return to the former way of life.

From your Anni

Three weeks later, Anni added in her diary:

Diary, February 21, 1932
What has happened during this time? It is all so tremendous and unfathomable. How to comprehend that the living God has come into life – into my life? We venture to ask him that we might be allowed to encounter him – to live a life of dedication and love after the example of his son, Jesus Christ. Who could ever have anticipated such a reality? ➤

Annemarie Wächter, a relative of the progressive educator Friedrich Froebel, grew up at the country boarding school in Keilhau, Germany that he had founded. After escaping to England from the Nazi regime in 1936 with her husband, a pacifist, she worked as an educator and counselor in the Bruderhof community in Rifton, New York until her death in 1980. These abridged selections were compiled by Marianne Wright.

"A community of people from the most varied classes and professions": Bruderhof members take a break from work (1932).

Janusz Korczak

JASON LANDSEL

"I am not here to be loved and admired. It is not the duty of people to help me, but it is my duty to look after the world and the people in it."

—*Janusz Korczak*

The date of birth for the Polish educator is unclear: a result of the fact that his father, a well-to-do Jewish citizen of Warsaw, delayed filling the birth registration paperwork (it was either 1878 or 1879). Also unclear is the date of Korczak's death, which – like that of millions of others murdered in Nazi extermination camps – went unrecorded. He was last seen on August 6, 1942 in Warsaw, when, having rejected repeated offers to escape, he accompanied a group of around two hundred Jewish orphans to the train that would take them to the Treblinka extermination camp.

As a young man, Korczak, whose real name was Henryk Goldszmit, was known for his sensitivity to the suffering of the marginalized. In particular, he seemed to be a magnet for street children, for whom he became a lifelong advocate as a doctor, author, and educator. Taking the nom de plume Janusz Korczak from a character in a children's story, he promoted his ideals of progressive education in a series of books that combined new insights from child psychology with straightforward love for children. As he wrote:

> Children are not the people of tomorrow, but people today. They are entitled to be taken seriously. They have a right to be treated by adults with tenderness and respect, as equals. They should be allowed to grow into whoever they were meant to be. . . . The unknown person inside each of them is the hope for the future.

Korczak was more than a theorist. In 1911, he and his co-worker Stefania Wilczynska established the Dom Sierot orphanage for Jewish children in Warsaw. As a creative environment where children could flourish, Korczak's orphanage even included the children's own parliament, court, and newspaper.

When the Nazis invaded Poland in 1939, Korczak was determined to protect his orphans and refused to go underground. Even when the children were interned in the Warsaw ghetto, he chose to stay with them: "You wouldn't abandon your own child in sickness, misfortune, or danger, would you? So how can I leave two hundred children now?" Starving and often ill, he spent the last two years of his life protecting his charges as best he could.

When in August 1942 the order came down for the orphans to be transported to Treblinka, Korczak and Wilczynska knew what it meant. Telling the children they were headed to a new home in the country, he led them in a festive procession to the train station, each child neatly dressed and carrying a favorite toy or book. In the words of one eyewitness: "I will never forget the sight to the end of my life. It was a silent but organized protest against the murders, a march which no human eye had ever seen before." The two teachers died with the children in the gas chambers shortly after their arrival in Treblinka.

Just days beforehand, Korczak had written in his diary: "I am angry with nobody. I do not wish anyone evil. I am unable to do so." ➤

Jason Landsel is the artist for Plough's *"Forerunners" series, including Janusz Korczak's portrait opposite.*

Sources: Janusz Korczak's *Ghetto Diary* (Yale University Press, 2003) and *When I Am Little Again* and *The Child's Right to Respect* (UPA, 1992); Betty Jean Lifton's *The King of Children: The Life and Death of Janusz Korczak* (St. Martin's Press, 1997).